Dewdrops on Stinging Nettles

A Companion for Practice

Tendo

Dewdrops on Stinging Nettles
A Companion for Practice

Revised and Expanded Edition, May 2025
First Edition June 2021
Copyright © 2025 by Robert j Kirkpatrick

Dream Mountain Press
6499 Wahl Rd.
Freeland WA 98249

ISBN-13: 979-8-218-60813-2
eBook: ISBN-13: 979-8-218-71614-1

Cover artwork by Andrew Woods

First Printing May 2025
10 9 8 7 6 5 4 3 2

DreamMountain.org

"Truth is a pathless land."
- J. Krishnamurti

Contents

Dewdrops

on

Stinging

Nettles

Beginnings

I constantly played outside when I was young—with friends when they'd come over—but more often, by myself. Some of the games I'd play would end with me lying on my back in the grass, "dead," staring up into the sky. When I was around nine or ten years of age, I began to linger there in the grass, just looking up into the sky for long stretches of time. I would gaze up into the rich blue sky in that golden period after the sun had set but when there was still plenty of light. As the light ebbed away and the stars brightened into view, I would be enveloped in this sense of timelessness. The barrier of separateness from our surroundings is much thinner at that age, but the process of lying there, gazing into the sky for extended periods of time, would erode any separateness until there was little sense of self. I can still remember how it felt when I would finally go inside: open, completely at ease, simply a presence moving through the house.

I would do this practice often in the next few years and continued to regularly engage with it well into my twenties. Sometimes I would lie down under grey cloudy skies, sometimes at other times of day, but always until the sense of self receded and there was only this vast openness. I never engaged in this endeavor for any sort of gain, or with any agenda, but as something I just did.

Within a year or two of beginning this practice, "sky gazing" we could call it, I turned that gaze inward toward memory, thoughts and habits. I had noticed certain tendencies cropping up, habits that I didn't understand where they had come from. I found certain sounds, activities, and behaviors increasingly difficult to tolerate. Why was that? What was the cause of this shift in my experience? I was determined to find out why, and so I began a process where I would dig through memory until I unearthed some root event, something that had precipitated that change. At that age, I was able to trace memory back to nearly the beginning of being able to form memories. I found that I was able to unearth root causes that would become habit and when I understood them, I was less controlled by them.

This process of questioning the self became a regular activity I would engage in. Typically, I would wedge myself into a small space, often facing a wall, and then I would question some action that I had taken until I found the source event. I tended to do this about once a year and I would try to come to a complete understanding of why I acted as I did. What event was at the heart of these behaviors? Was my response justified? In essence, I was questioning who I really was. Are we nothing more than a loose collection of habits?

It would be a far stretch to say that my teenage years were dominated by self investigation, but this remained a part of my core behavior and a skill that I turned upon what I was taught in all spheres. By the time I was finished with high school, I had rejected established explanations on the nature of reality and was convinced that I had to see for myself *"what was really going on."*

While remaining concerned with this existential question, it was many years before I would take on a formal investigation, a practice. Once I had set off on such a path, I soon committed myself to putting the practice first among all my activities. But I quickly found that the organizations and systems that purported to support such endeavors were rarely in accord with that approach. I had made the commitment but I found that I wasn't engaged in a full time practice at all. This was the first seed of the Dream Mountain approach.

The solution that I conceived of was to develop a body of practices that one could use in addition to whatever system of formal practice one was engaged in. This would be a program of continuous practice, integrating it into all aspects of one's life. It wasn't until my practice had flowered to the point that I discovered the gazing practices that I was able to fully enact this program. By now, I had found an approach to myriad methods, both traditional and novel, that in their entirety, formed a complete practice regime. Thus the Dream Mountain Way was born.

§

Practice, in virtually all of its forms, is oriented around answering that question of *"what is really going on?"* and, just as essentially, *"how do we embody our understanding?"* The tools of practice in all their myriad varieties can be divided into two broad categories: cultivating openness and investigation. Along with bringing a correct attitude toward practice, these form a three legged stool of practice.

The first part of this book presents the Foundations upon which practice is based. Here we present various facets of the right attitude that one takes to genuinely engage with the practice. We begin with the **Perspective** that this approach takes toward both our condition and the attitude that facilitates practice.

The following section, **Cultivating the Still Pool**, presents methods of contemplation that facilitate ever expansive openness. We present the core metaphor of the still pool, which the open mind embodies. With the **Gazing** practices we venture outside and use all of our senses to further cultivate openness and begin to probe into the barriers we have erected that keep us closed and separate.

We turn our gaze inwards in the **Investigation** section as we tackle numerous approaches where we engage directly with mind. In **Continuous Practice**, we see how the three legged stool of practice is used in myriad activities throughout all aspects of our life. Finally we conclude with **Patterning**, where we try to give some sense to that which is beyond words.

§

This is a book of practices that was written in the midst of practice. That is to say, it is not written from the perspective of one at the far reaches of a long path of training, trying to relate to those in the middle of their journey. This is a perspective that can be of great value to those of us still in the throes of practice, the perspective of the good friend. In this book, I offer approaches to techniques both familiar and novel. There is a lot of nuance to the methods that we engage with and explanations are always insufficient, always a bit vague. This book is no different. Throughout, I have presented in a simple and direct manner, methods that have proven to enhance and deepen our practice. With sufficient time and attention, we can put down the barriers that separate us from what is really going on and see it for ourselves.

Tendo
Tahoma Zen Monastery
Spring 2025

Foundations

Perspective

The problems and concerns that vex us can seem insurmountable, especially when considering the obstacles that confront us. Tried and true tactics and strategies seem unequal to the times, compromised by use and those who dismiss and undermine them. However considering the consequences of inaction, of the inability to enact desperately needed change, there is a growing urgency.

The failure to confront the issues that have grown into crisis and that seem so overwhelming spring from attempting change at the level of society instead of the individual. The root of our problems, from the individual through to society, arise from our identification with that which is transient, conditioned and provisional, that is the self. The self is merely a construction of memory, conditioning and ever shifting emotions, mental states and impulses. When we identify with this construction we are in thrall to its efforts to preserve itself, grasping after what sustains it and pushing away that which undermines it.

The essence of practice, of all practice, is to engage in activities that reveal the ephemerality of the self and ultimately bring about its end, while opening us up to what is real. As we engage with practice, we become ever open, increasingly flexible, and better able to respond to circumstances. As we operate less and less from the self and more and more from *reality as is*, we operate for the benefit of all beings, for we see how we are all connected, how we all have the same nature. It is only this–the free, open and flexible individual that operates from the perspective of totality that is able to respond effectively to the challenges that arise.

The Dream Mountain Way

There are no masters of the Dream Mountain Way—no hierarchy, no organization, no temples, no rituals, no authority. But there are many teachers—clouds, oceans, trees, mountains, rocks, rivers, dragonflies, the night sky, owls, the setting sun, boundless plains, ravens, deep blue skies, butterflies, silence and subtle words and, of course, good friends. We return to these again and again in the practice; they can always be relied upon to keep our feet firmly planted on the path.

There are no sacred spaces, or more accurately, we can recognize the sacred in every place. We practice wherever circumstances place us, but we emphasize environments where the close observation of natural processes facilitates the course of our practices. In this way, we find places that resonate with us and, recognizing that this will differ for everyone, we don't make any claims of universality. But those places of resonance–meadows, mountains, lakes, backyards, seaside paths, parks, city streets–these sustain us, guide us and keep us on our path. These environments are where we go to meet so many of our teachers, and engage in myriad practices. Without objectification, without striving for specialness, we are open and grateful to these places that resonate with us, that hold our hearts.

Good Friends

All those who are navigating the path are able to point toward the path; all followers of the way can gesture toward their circuitous route. Those who have gazed deeply, seen into the nature of things, can also be relied upon to provide perspective. These good friends will gesture toward the way, reminding us that it has no end, no destination, and that all paths must eventually be abandoned. Good friends can provide needed encouragement, subtle words, reality checks or tools at the opportune moment.

Likewise, we ourselves are called upon to be good friends, in turn. For we all have something to share, and are able to point toward the path we have trod. We are honest about where we are on the way—a fellow good friend—making no claims of authority. We are grateful for our good friends and express that gratitude in helping as we are able.

Orientation

These matters must be approached with an orientation toward truth, fairness and kindness. The rule of thumb that we adopt in our interactions with others is one of empathy: treat others as we ourselves would like to be treated. This orientation, which is a simple set of guidelines for living in an ethical manner, grounds us in this process of finding our way.

In the search for deeper truths, we must be completely committed to truth itself. Being honest with ourselves and with others is where this begins. A fundamental sense of fairness in our interactions with others reduces the frictions between people, frictions that add barriers to the search for truth. The near universal maxims to treat others as we ourselves would like to be treated and to not treat others as we would not like to be treated provides heuristics in our interactions with others. Finally, be kind. We should be kind to ourselves and to others.

Each of us makes our own path and we all find our own approach to these matters. These simple guidelines provide the framework to keep our footing in a process that questions everything, pushes past all boundaries and requires the letting go of all which we hold onto. In this process, we still interact with others and it is essential that the practice not be used as an excuse to further distance ourselves. Indeed, as we follow the twists and turns of the path, we will find that our orientation shifts further from our sense of self, toward others, toward all things. In the end, the practice leads to the embodiment of the questions, *what is true?*, and, *how, then, do we live?*

A Pathless Path

There is no single path, no royal road that encompasses all beings. Indeed there is no path to be found. It is only by looking backward at the unique features of any given person's experience that we can identify something we would call a path. The Dream Mountain Way is thus to provide the tools that each individual can pick up and put to use as circumstances demand. These practices can be used individually to supplement an existing methodology, or can be used as a complete program. They are not set in stone and are presented with the understanding that each person will find their own approach to using them as best fits their current conditions.

The Dream Mountain Way takes as its foundation that every individual is a unique expression of *reality as is* and will respond accordingly to circumstances in unique and unpredictable ways. Thus, it is presented as a series of practices with the explicit understanding that everyone will trace a different course through these practices, using what works in any given moment. Furthermore, the way that each individual will take up any given practice–make it work for them–is also unique. A good friend can help us on the path but ultimately, our journey is our own.

What's Really Going On

Fundamental reality is one of infinite connections, everything dependent upon everything else, all in constant flux. From the smallest particle to the largest object, from the most subtle feeling to the most grandiose thought, all are subject to change; all things are born and pass away. Ultimately there is nothing fixed, nothing permanent, nothing that exists independently of everything else. This practice that we engage in, is so that we can reconnect to this natural way of being and shed this sense we have that we are separate, that we are independent, and in our deepest of thoughts, that we are permanent. The Dream Mountain Way is a collection of devices that we can use to bring us to a place where we can see what is really going on for ourselves, for no concepts, no words can adequately get at it. Anything of the self is ultimately distancing, always dividing the world. The practice leads us to see through the false notion of a separate self, to unbind that which is preventing us from genuine freedom. It is not a matter of faith; it is a process that we must undergo to encounter *reality as is.*

Wayseeking Mind

Wayseeking Mind is the need to know, *what is this?, what is true?, what is real?, who am I?, what is really going on?* and most essentially, *what is birth?,* and *what is death?* Coming to the path for any other reason is a perfectly understandable and often wondrous thing. During the course of practice, self-oriented goals can fall away. Wayseeking Mind can be roused. Most people have these hints of what's real, like a memory of a taste, or scenting faint traces of perfume still lingering in an empty room. Even just the receding of the self for a moment, sinking into deep absorption, or coming out of a period of contemplation with more energy than with which we started is like a thread into *what is.* When we sense this thread and pull on it, self-oriented motivations fall away: escaping suffering, finding peace, self-improvement, being more balanced, improving our health and so on. We pull on that thread and wonder, *what is this? What is true?* Finding out becomes the most important thing.

Commitment

The absolute root of our practice is commitment– commitment to constantly return our attention to the practice, commitment to bringing our practice into lived experience, commitment to not increasing the suffering in the world, and commitment to responding as circumstances demand. Therefore, we engage in the practice in every activity, wherever we are, twenty-four hours a day. There are no "breaks" from the practice; can we take a break from living our life?

Commitment goes hand in hand with trust, trust in this practice. As we follow the various techniques outlined herein and find that they change how we see things, how we experience things, and how we engage in the world, our trust grows. As our trust grows, we become increasingly confident in the practice and in our engagement with it. Our commitment grows along with it. There is a point where we see that we are not isolated, separate agents operating to maximize our personal benefits but that, in fact, there is only *what is*. Our conditioning may result in this being a temporary occurrence, but it changes us forever. It is true freedom, away from self-orientation, away from trying to hold onto things that are inherently in flux, away from the dissatisfaction with this ever-changing world. When this occurs, we want nothing more than for everyone to live this way and our commitment becomes total.

Effective Practice

Truth is a pathless land, but additionally, it is a path without a destination. Reality continuously unfolds, revealing ever greater nuance and depth. When we simply practice without a goal, this endless unfolding is a source of wonder and joy. This orientation towards a practice that accepts not knowing has three primary facets: confidence, engagement and uncertainty.

Confidence

When we work though myriad practices, giving them time and attention, our confidence in the practice grows. This is so because we find that practices oriented around focusing our minds, relaxing our bodies and opening our awareness does indeed cultivate a more focused mind, relaxed body and open awareness. When the results are as described, we see that the methods have valency and are worthy of our trust. As our confidence increases, we are able to put down our small doubts, let go of an (initially) healthy skepticism and simply practice. This empirically oriented approach, grounded in our own experience, forms a firm foundation that allows us to delve much deeper into long-term forms of investigation. For without trust in our methods, we are unable to give ourselves wholly to them.

Engagement

As our confidence grows, so does our willingness and ability to completely engage in whatever practice we are working on. Whatever may bring us to engage in a practice, at the moment we take it up, we put down everything else. There is only the practice. Our engagement with our practice leads to more effective practice, which increases our confidence in our practice, which leads us to greater and greater engagement with the practice. Confidence and engagement are inextricably linked and fuel each other.

Deeper practice demands complete engagement. The structures that support our sense of separation from what is really going on are the only reality we know. To question these and see their limits cannot be done half-heartedly. Blind trust is not the Dream Mountain Way and thus, it is not expected of us. Total engagement is only possible when we are able to accept risk. To engage with *what is*, is not without risk and a foundation of trust is essential. Upon that foundation, total commitment is possible and from there, we can cast ourselves into the unknown.

Uncertainty

When we are able to engage completely with our method for sustained periods of time, at some point, we will begin to cultivate an existential uncertainty. This is where the practice leads, to the essential questions of *what is true* and *how then do we live?* These are the concerns that are at the root of all questions, of all practice: the questions of life and death. There is nothing but uncertainty around these fundamental concerns and the path of practice is directed toward resolving these questions. When there is great uncertainty, it is a physical experience, a great weight in the body and it is all-consuming. All other small questions, doubts, and anxiety are subsumed in this great uncertainty. When this great mass of uncertainty is smashed through, the matter is resolved.

If we approach the practice in this way, toward total engagement, toward the cultivation of uncertainty, then it can be adapted to all circumstances. While there is value to situations that allow for us to practice with little concern for daily activities, it is not a prerequisite. What matters is that we have confidence in the practice and when we pick up a method, our engagement is total. All of the circumstances of our ordinary lives are fuel for cultivating uncertainty.

Letting Go

It is the nature of the practice that it stirs up intense emotions as the bonds of conditioning are revealed. The circumstances of our lives in general always challenge us and it is our response to these events that form this conditioning. Societal, unconscious and formative conditioning can be repressed, buried, forgotten or obscured. We learn to function in the world as distant, isolated egos protecting ourselves by further distancing ourselves and dividing the world into self and other. So as this becomes revealed, as things long-buried or repressed come to the fore, as we experience new challenging circumstances, this can be overwhelming to our more open self. Our barriers are lower and we feel things more directly. Since the self still remains, and is far more open, it is much more vulnerable. Thus, the circumstances of the world, the traumas, slights, incongruities and myriad forms of suffering affect us more deeply, cut to the marrow. How we face these circumstances, how we respond to these wounds, this is an essential component of the practice.

There are approaches that we take to the arising of intense thoughts, feelings and emotions. When strong feelings arise, we open ourselves to them and feel them fully. We don't suppress them, cut them off, try to think of something else, try to ignore them or employ any other form of disengagement. We acknowledge the feelings, and accept them for what they are, thereby giving them space to arise. As they arise, we do not shy away from them or suppress them. We feel them fully in the body. The essential thing is that this is an embodied practice. The feelings will often increase in intensity but at some point, they will release. Then we return to our practice.

It is important not to wallow in these thoughts, feelings and emotions, gnawing on them over and over again. We let them come to the surface, feel them entirely and then let them release. This is a process of engaging, working through, and letting go of attachments. Deep-seated issues may require going through this process multiple times, but always as they naturally arise.

This is a truly fruitful practice for working through our conditioning which is what so much of the practice is about. We cultivate openness to give space for our feelings and manifestations of our conditioning to arise. We engage in investigation to reveal, expose and sever the bonds of attachments. Over and over again, we expose our conditioning and let it go until only openness remains.

Questioning the Self

As we engage in this practice, we find that we are often standing in our own way. That is, our likes and dislikes, inclinations, memories, habits, beliefs, feelings, foibles and other mental constructions will be barriers that we have to overcome. The practice will stir these up and it is incumbent upon us to know how to work our way through what can be traumatic occurrences. This is the process of letting go. But in conjunction with this, we should investigate and find the roots of what we have constructed: our false sense of a separate self. This process is undertaken by questioning the self.

We begin this by questioning things that we already are aware of: habits we feel controlled by, our particular forms of reactivity that cause so many problems, personality quirks we wish we weren't so pushed around by. Why do we react in this way? This needs to be thoroughly investigated. This can be done in stillness-sitting, or simply in any place of isolation, or even while engaged in physical activity.

The process is to pick one of these habits, reactions or behaviors and relentlessly question it until we find the root cause. Trace back to the initiating event. This may cause intense emotion in some cases:

shame, fear, pain, loneliness and other intense feelings we shy away from. But some of our grasping behavior may have arisen from situations that gave us joy, delight, or happiness. The process is to identify the foundation, to face it, and feel the resulting emotions in the body. Our bodies can handle these emotions no matter how intense they get. Eventually, they will release and we will accept these events, feelings, traumas for what they are, and then we can let them go. We may have to repeat this over and over for deeply-buried experiences. This may have to be done in a more concentrated way, in stillness-sitting, to truly delve into buried or repressed feelings.

Beneath behaviors, habits and feelings, we can find root beliefs that are entangled with memories and events and can be long-held, including notions of self worth, core fears, and strong concepts of identity. If we can discover these, often the shock of recognition can allow us to let them go, taking with these false beliefs much of the associated conditioning.

As we work through this process, we can tackle increasingly subtle forms of conditioning. In stillness-sitting, what is our baseline feeling? Is it one of equanimity? If not, we investigate what we are feeling. Are we feeling discontented, anxious, disoriented, miserable, distant, or apathetic? Trace that to its root. Are we suppressing feelings or are we perhaps indulging in our feelings? What is the root belief that lies at the core of that behavior? In the end, all of this is in support of our notion of an isolated, individual self. As we work through these feelings and associated beliefs, we remove those supports and as the practice creates the conditions to drop past the self, it becomes increasingly unable to reconstitute itself.

Cultivating the Still Pool

Cultivating the Still Pool

Becoming like a perfectly still pool—reflecting everything and nothing, no distinction between interior and exterior—this is the nature of this practice. There are numerous ways into this modality: following the breath, relaxing into awareness, intensive investigation and the myriad gazing practices. This orientation is one of naturalness: being in our body, following its lead, flowing effortlessly without engaging the self. The question of effort is a vital one. Whenever there is effort, the will is engaged and the will is the functioning of the self. But we can use effort to establish a practice, over time relaxing the use of self-directed effort, and becoming ever more natural.

When engaged in stillness-sitting, we must be relaxed and open, and cultivate a sense of equanimity. If we are grasping after thoughts or states, and rejecting feelings or sensations, our minds are tense and disturbed. When thoughts arise, we notice this, and check our body for tension and ease it wherever we find it. We relax even the placing of our gaze and settle into an awareness of our entire body sitting. When we are just sitting, thoughts pour away like water and we rest in openness.

When we relax into openness, especially when we

take that final step of relaxing our gaze, we are cultivating the still pool. There are no concerns of the
self, no agenda, or technique, just our entire being
engaged in sitting. Just as with effort, we can employ
very basic techniques such as breath-guided relaxation, to reach a place where we let go of method.
That place is the still pool.

The still pool is bottomless, all the way down to
reality as is. We can sink down into the still pool until
we are fully plunged into original nature. We can drop
questions in and see what emerges. And at times, we
can just dive right in and break through to the limit-
less depths.

Relaxing into openness can lead us right down into
original nature. We relax the body until we have no
sense of it; we relax our gaze until there is only
awareness; we relax our thinking until there is only
silence. This is cultivating the still pool. When this
becomes natural and we settle into the still pool without effort, without thought, dwelling nowhere, we
become ever more open to *what is*.

Stillness Sitting

Stillness-sitting, in all its diverse forms, is a core method for investigation. Stillness in our body is reflected in our minds and thus is a prerequisite for sustained practice. Stability is essential and it is the basis of posture, but posture is not the practice; it is simply a tool we use in order to enhance investigation. In the Dream Mountain Way, we sit anywhere: on a tree stump in the woods, on a bench waiting for the bus, on a log at the seashore, on a cushion in a practice setting, on a rock at the mountaintop, on the front stoop of an apartment and anywhere else that we can sit. Even sitting is not essential. We can stand still and engage in many of these practices, and when walking, we are not separate from stillness. Thus as we consider more formal approaches, note the essence and how that can be manifested in any situation.

When we sit on a cushion, chair, stump, or rock, we position ourselves in a posture such that we can maintain our position for an extended period of time. We form a tripod with our knees or feet and sit-bones. We sit comfortably erect, shoulders back, nose vertical, eyes horizontal. We settle into this posture, perhaps swaying side-to-side and back-and-forth, finding our natural center of gravity. Rooting ourselves, we sink into the base of our posture, sink into earth. We relax the whole body, easing any tension. Breath-guided relaxation codifies this method, guiding us in releasing the stress and tightness we have built up. Then we simply remain still.

There is an energy that flows from stillness, relaxing ourselves, skin to bone, relaxing even our attention. Naturally, the mind mirrors the body, thoughts pouring away. The longer we sit in this stillness, the deeper we can relax and let go.

Our breath follows this pattern as well; unforced, and at ease, it naturally deepens. When our breath is ragged, gasping, rapid or erratic in any other way, we cannot be still. We settle the breath by placing our awareness upon our abdomen just below the navel. Our attention there, we breathe from the abdomen, diaphragmatically, unforced and ever deeper, ever gentler.

Our thoughts follow the stillness of our bodies and breath. We move our awareness from the settled breath to our baseline feeling. If we are agitated, or anxious in any way, that will dominate our thoughts directly or unconsciously. Equanimity is the baseline of stillness-sitting. We may need to probe into our anxieties to let them go, but sometimes we can just acknowledge them and subtly change the conditions and flow into equanimity. Sometimes sitting with the trace of a smile on our faces is enough to cause this shift. Noting any residual tenseness anywhere in our body and simply placing our awareness there can be enough to change the conditions such that equanimity naturally arises. We return to, or initiate, breath-guided relaxation as necessary.

Stillness of body, mind and breath points toward quiescence and awareness of vast space. It is in this space where there is the potential to gaze into thoughts, sounds, and sights, to be open to *what is*, and to probe deep into experience, until only *reality as is* remains.

Breath Guided Relaxation

When stillness-sitting, we sit comfortably erect, back straight and naturally curved, eyes level, nose vertical, chin tucked in. Shoulders should be slightly back, arms slightly open, hands resting in our lap. Eyes should be just slightly open. We settle into our seat, rooted.

For each breath, we naturally exhale until we automatically inhale. There should be no effort involved. We place attention upon the abdomen and feel its rising and falling. The breath will, of its own accord, deepen and lengthen as we relax. We settle into the breath, solid and rooted. We place our awareness upon a portion of the body and ease downward over the duration of the exhalation. We naturally inhale and check again for tension in the target area, repeating as necessary. In the procedure, we follow our breath always downwards, starting from the top of the head until we reach the soles of the feet.

The face is a particularly tense part of the body and we give it time, relaxing the forehead, eyes, cheeks and jaw. We turn up the corners of the mouth, settling the small muscles of the face. When the tension has eased, we move to the neck, shoulders and arms. This is a region of the body that can be especially tight, so it can be helpful to tense the shoulder muscles and then let them release, again following the breath. The next area we move our awareness to is the chest and abdomen, following the breath downwards, into the lower abdomen, the center of gravity.

The next region is the upper, middle and lower back. Once we have given these areas our time and attention, we sink down to the hips and allow our weight to settle into our sit bones. We sit like a tree, rooted in the earth, back like the straight trunk, our head level and balanced at the crown. Sway side to side and back and forth like a tree in the wind, finding the natural balance point. Then, following the breath we move awareness down the hips, thighs, knees and calves to the feet. Fully relaxed, we return our awareness to the top of the head and let it pour down the entire body, checking for any remaining tension, dwelling for a few breaths where any is found.

Every time we engage in stillness-sitting, we should be relaxed, always beginning with breath-guided relaxation. As our sitting continues, we can tense up from trying to avoid discomfort, or from the arising of thoughts, emotions and sensations. We are attentive to these shifts and we direct our gaze upon areas of tension. A few breaths should ease any remaining tightness. Instead of shying away from discomfort, we relax into it, avoiding any attempt to separate ourselves from what is really going on.

As we settle into our practice, we may not need to dedicate as much time to the full relaxation process. Instead, we isolate those areas we find particularly tense: face, shoulders, hips—everyone's areas of tension will differ—and focus on just these regions until any tension releases. Then we simply continue with stillness-sitting.

Focus

It is vital to be able to place our awareness, to naturally let energy flow to a single point, concentrating our scattered minds. Through practice, we can develop this skill which is the crux of so many methods.

The ability to focus our awareness upon an object, be it in the environment, in our bodies or in our mind, is essential to engage in many practices. But it also is a practice in and of itself. A focused mind is not filled with scattered thoughts, and ultimately is empty of a sense of self. This unified mind—the One Mind—is empty awareness. But as with any practice, there are risks of grasping and using it to sustain the sense of a separate self. When fully absorbed, body and mind fall away and we dwell in the object of focus. We may find this restful, an escape from the business of our thoughts and the grasping of the self. But when we stand up, we are no longer in this deep concentration and that peace is gone. There is no unity with practice and ordinary activity. This is not the One Mind. Thus, we develop focus as a tool and work with the rest of the practices toward seeing through the illusion of self.

We begin as always–relaxed, cultivating the still pool, shifting our awareness to our abdomen, feeling the rise and fall of the breath. It is vital that this is the focus, that we remain alert and attentive to the breath moving through our bodies. Naturalness is equally essential; we don't force the breath or, by will, attempt to control it. We simply keep our awareness directed toward the abdomen. Thoughts may arise; we are attentive of them, acknowledging them for what they are, and then returning awareness back to the breath. If we notice that we have followed a thought for a period of time, we do not comment upon this or castigate ourselves for being off-method, we simply return our awareness to the breath. If our thoughts are too scattered to stay with our breath in this manner, we employ strategies that require ever more attention. Counting exhalations from one to ten is the most basic. When necessary, we can increase the complexity of counting by counting by twos, by odd numbers, backwards and so on. We do this to engage the conceptual mind until it settles down. Then we simply place our awareness on the rise and fall of the abdomen.

In this way, we build up the skills of noticing when we are unfocused, of placing our awareness without commentary, and over time, we develop ever deeper concentration.

In the same way that we can transition from the still pool into openness, we can move from focusing on the breath into openness. When we engage in a period of stillness-sitting, we always begin by relaxing and settling into the still pool. Once settled, we place our awareness on the abdomen as it rises and falls. If our minds are particularly scattered, we engage in the necessary breath-counting practice. As it calms down, we return our gaze to the movement of the abdomen, always focusing awareness there when we are distracted. As distractions fall away, we simply increase the field of our awareness from the rise and fall of the abdomen to our entire bodies and from there, expand to include our surroundings, increasingly open.

Every time that we engage in stillness-sitting, we should transition into openness. Until focus is deeply developed, this might just be for short periods of time; we return to the breath as we lose focus. But the practice of focus, like all of the practices, leads to increased openness, bringing us into greater resonance with *what is*.

Openness

Openness is our natural condition, a condition that the barrier of the self has created an illusory separation from. Openness can't be forced; we must ease into it naturally. We become increasingly open by cultivating the still pool and settling into awareness of our entire bodies. Then we can open up further by listening, letting sounds in without discrimination, without placing attention on them. This brings our sense of awareness beyond ourselves.

Likewise, the gazing practices bring us to a place of greater and greater openness. Using the channels of eyes and ears and skillfully applying focus, we become in tune with the landscape that is in our visual and auditory sensorium.

With practice, we become increasingly open, open to sounds, sights, and sensations, open to our bodies and surroundings, open to *what is*. By not chasing thoughts, by not naming or commenting upon what we see and hear, by not indulging in sensations, by not forcing everything into our story, we open ever further and we effortlessly remain open. Thoughts simply rise and fall, uncommented upon and over time, diminish. Our narrative fades and our sense of a separate self recedes. It is in this open condition, where we are mostly just a presence in landscape, that our modality is simply empty awareness. We find ourselves increasingly in tune with *what is*.

Feelings come and go; thoughts pour away; the sense of self diminishes, and is revealed to be ultimately empty. Our mind like a mirror, a clear still pool reflecting landscape, an empty vast silence. No separation.

Opening to Totality

Operating from openness puts us into alignment with *what is* and provides space for investigation into thoughts, feelings and beliefs. Openness is our natural functioning. How we move through the world. In the course of our practice, we become increasingly open until we reach a place where there are no obstructions.

In order to aid this cultivation, we can use a technique of engaging with our imagination. Through the skillful use of our imagination, guided by words, we develop a sense of increasing openness. As with any use of mental activity, this is a temporary expedient to help us develop a feel—a sense of what we are trying to cultivate. Once we have embodied this sense, we can simply open until this becomes seamless, that is, dwelling in totality, without limit.. Finally this dwelling itself can be put down until the functioning is *reality as is,* constantly changing, vibrantly interconnected and unobstructed. *Non-dwelling.*

Guided Imagining

In stillness-sitting, we begin with breath-guided relaxation. Once we have settled our body and mind, we turn our awareness to our breath, to the rise and fall of the abdomen. We abide with that sensation for a few breaths and then, we expand our awareness to a sense of our whole body. We see our body sitting in this room as if we're looking down on it from above. We expand our openness to include the room we are sitting in, the space and everything in it.

We expand this awareness beyond the immediate space to the structure we are in, open to all that lies within.

We open ourselves to the surrounding neighborhood and all that it contains–landscape, beings, objects.

We expand our awareness to the whole county taking it all in–buildings, people, animals, plants, everything.

Next, we open to the entire region and its myriad activities and entities.

The whole country–all of these beings, things, landscapes in all their complexity; we drink them down.

We open to the hemisphere and take it all in, excluding nothing whatsoever, seamless.

We visualize the earth. We see the whole earth; we are aware of all of its many, many individual interconnected beings.

We open up to encompass our solar system, with

all its planets and myriad objects and beings they contain and all the space between.

Now the entire galaxy with its numerous stars, planets, entities and uncountable phenomenon.

We open to the entire universe, everything that exists at this moment.

We open ourselves to all possible realms in the past, present and future. We open to all possibilities, all things in all moments in all conditions and states of being.

We notice at this time the deep, abiding silence. We find all of these myriad things dwelling in that stillness. Any thoughts, feelings, or emotions are just part of this totality. If they arise, they arise. We simply return to *what is*. If our eyes are open, we see this totality in whatever our gaze falls upon. There is no obstruction, in the phenomenon in our gaze, in all phenomena. In wandering thoughts, all things. *Totality.*

We dwell in this totality. We familiarize ourselves with it. Then we let even that go; there is only the suchness of the totality of all phenomena: *reality as is.*

Non-Dwelling

While there is reason and value to dwell in openness, increasingly engaged with *what is*, the condition of the awakened mind is one of non-dwelling. Our normal view is from the self; we dwell in this sense of separateness, that we are this and everything else is that. The mind of freedom is not in such a static viewpoint. It is the energetic, generative, continual transformation that is reality. In the midst of thought, no-thought. We can practice this in stillness-sitting, but also beyond this, in all our activities. In any action, we aren't attached to any particular view or outcome. Thus, we are able to respond freely.

When gazing into entangled complexity, or interpenetration, or dancing randomness, this is where our grasping selves can find no purchase, no place to rest. These are non-dwelling practices, where our mind is alert, open and endlessly transformative.

Questioning, where no answer is accepted, and we question all that arises, is a practice of non-dwelling. The sense of uncertainty is no place to dwell, yet we cultivate it. It is in flux, keeping us on our back foot, unstable. Even as it becomes all encompassing, roiling, like a sense of waiting, beyond all expectations. When this shatters, the self collapses and then, we truly abide nowhere.

When stillness-sitting the practice of opening to totality is a non-dwelling practice when there is no resting in any place of openness. There is no destination in openness, no endpoint. It is an infinity of infinities, beyond the grasp of our conceptual minds. Alert, open, still, not in any way tense or restless, we are an expression of that infinity of infinities, constantly in flux, responding to circumstances as they manifest.

Wherever we find ourselves, whatever activity we are engaged in, we approach it with this alertness, taking everything in all-at-once. Resting anywhere is the abode of the self, reinforcing the illusion of separateness. Empty awareness is the condition of the mind that dwells nowhere.

In stillness-sitting, with body relaxed, breath settled, open, we let go of any place where we would dwell. We settle into the breath for an exhalation or two, then put down the breath. We listen to our environment, opening up to our surroundings, then put down hearing. We let go of the past and the future. Eyes open, the ground beneath our gaze a blur, we put down sight. Likewise, we put down smell, taste and touch. Feelings arise; we put them down. The sense of equanimity–we let it go. Desires, sensations– we set them aside. What has brought us to practice, our motivation, our will—we put them down. Thoughts arise and we notice them, notice we are not separate from them. We let them go. Increasingly open, that sense of openness—we put it down.

We notice when we are settling into anything—thoughts, feelings, perceptions, impulses, instinct, sensation, concepts, practices, states of mind, openness, awareness—we let them all go. We are simply aware of dwelling and we set it aside. No commentary, no thoughts, no conceptualization. We notice and let go. Then even that, we let go.

Gazing

Gazing

In the gazing practices, we engage with our surroundings such that we don't project ourselves into the world. Instead, we see what is in our sensory field as shining into us. The practice of gazing is being fully open to where attention has been placed. We stay with the subject of attention without labeling, discriminating or commenting upon it. If such language arises, we let it naturally pour away. We simply are open to what is in the field of view. We allow this openness to persist for a sustained duration. Time, which is inextricable from thought, will flow away, as thoughts flow away. As attention releases, awareness opens up. We let this naturally occur. Very gently, seamlessly gazing, this widens from dwelling upon our field of view into an open awareness.

We gaze inwardly, placing our attention upon the breath and expanding out to our entire body until it opens to awareness. We can gaze externally at what is in our field of view until it gently ebbs into open awareness. This practice of gazing follows from focus: diffused attention opening up focus into awareness. It is necessary to be able to seamlessly shift from focus into gazing and to let go of the distinction. Gazing externally is fundamentally a natural practice oriented toward empty awareness. When we walk, we walk from our bodies, in awareness. Over time, we find we don't need to think about where we are going or what we are doing. The constant narration falls silent and we are just a presence moving within our surroundings, which are simply a collection of processes, each a singular expression of *reality as is*.

When we stop and let things go and open up our senses, we are practicing maintaining that functioning without the filtering of our conditioned responses. We are training ourselves to remain in openness. Gazing is practicing seeing the world as it truly is, being fully open to *what is*.

Silence

There is a hush that falls around sunset, in that golden time of twilight. The birds cease their constant activity and noise, people retreat to their houses, and the activities of the daylight hours draw to a close. The very world seems still. It is a valuable practice to sit outside during this time, sitting comfortably or lying on the ground gazing up into the sky or out into the landscape. Stillness deepens. If we devote enough time to this endeavor, a sense of the deep silence behind the stillness manifests.

In our stillness-sitting, whether indoors or outdoors, as we cultivate the still pool, we become increasingly aware of this deep, essential silence. Notice this silence and open up to it. When sounds arise, we observe how they emerge from this silence and decay back into it. The silence is at the root of all of these sounds; it is the essence.

Likewise, our thoughts arise out of this silence, spin themselves out, then fall back into it. We watch this closely without commentary, without indulging the thoughts, and without cutting them off. The transitory nature of these thoughts becomes apparent; the silence is what remains. It teaches us, and nourishes us. It absorbs our inner shouts, demands, questions, feelings and concerns. With close enough observation, we find that we are no longer hearing sounds or silence, but are simply hearing. This has its own silence, distinct from the arbitrary distinction we make between sound and silence. This is awareness, the experience of hearing itself. We open to this and the awareness grows diffuse, not the awareness of hearing, but awareness in and of itself, the field in which all senses resolve. In this openness, there is no discrimination of this sense data—no sounds, no silence, no sights, no seeing, no feeling. There is only increasing openness, a vast active silence, fully alert, dynamic, and non-dwelling.

We fully immerse ourselves in this silence, ever deeper into the still pool, into the very essence in which there is only this silence.

Being Outside

When out of doors, we are naturally in our bodies.
By being aware of our bodies—awareness in our center of gravity, rooting ourselves in the earth, breathing naturally—we can truly inhabit them. As we move
amidst the natural environment with all its continual
change, we become increasingly aware of silence. Behind every sound, behind the incessant activity, is a
deep silence. At twilight, when birds come to rest and
people are generally not out and about, we can feel a
hushed stillness, that points to a yet deeper
silence. Paying attention to these conditions facilitates
seeing past the self.

When sitting out of doors, our movement, often
noisy and careless, disturbs our surroundings. Stillness-sitting out of doors integrates us into the surroundings, and the wildlife that our rough behavior
alienates, becomes increasingly comfortable in our
presence. Birds will fly right by; small mammals scur-
ry up to check us out; deer amble by, unconcerned
with our presence. As our stillness matures, we become just another feature of the landscape. We spend
much of our lives distancing ourselves from our surroundings and in this way, become a disturbance
when we move through our environment. Being still

outside teaches us how to naturally move through our environment again.

When we are seated outside, or where we can see the outdoors, this is not an opportunity to "watch" or to attach to additional stimulus. Gazing at *what is* in our field of view is not different from gazing at the floor in front of us. We engage in outdoor sitting in order to facilitate empty awareness.

We sit as we normally would, eyes mostly closed, head level, but gaze cast downward. Let the sounds of the outdoors, which will increase as we become ever more still, flow through us. We let go of the environment and relax into awareness, cultivating the still pool. When thoughts have subsided, we open our eyes, fully utilizing our peripheral vision. There should be no distinction between them being open or closed. The still pool, deeply clear, undisturbed by thought, sensations and feelings, brightly mirrors all that shines in.

Alternatively, we can sit with eyes open but not focused on anything. In this manner, we are using the complexity of the environment to move past the self. Things can appear as a blur, or almost like static. If we are able to, we sit somewhere where in our direct view, is something complex, like a stand of trees, or a mass of shrubs. We simply relax our whole body, especially the eyes, keeping them open. If a bird or in-

sect flies by, we let it enter and exit our field of view without naming it, commenting upon it or dwelling upon it. If a thought arises, we notice this and let it fall away without pursuing it, commenting upon it or dwelling upon it. We notice when we do label, or comment upon things and let go of that train of thought, simply returning to our gazing.

In this way, our field of view, the very landscape, feeds into the cultivation of empty awareness.

Sky Gazing

We lie down outside in the grass or on some surface and gaze up into the sky. A solid grey mass is its own form of emptiness, as is the transparent depths of a clear blue sky. Scattered clouds amidst a deep blue sky are rife with fractal edges, endless dimensions, layered complexities and gaps revealing connections. Gazing with eyes wide, with our peripheral vision, into whatever form the sky takes, our mind settles, opening into awareness. We take it in all at once. Wandering thoughts are subsumed into the vastness, the depths of the sky. This is the sky as the still pool.

Deepening this practice is a function of staying with it. Laying down, looking into the sky, for an hour or longer opens ourselves up completely. Our endless narrative is subsumed in the deep sky. As we lie there, we can use the complexity of the clouds to diminish this chatter; we can bring all our attention to those small gaps of emptiness, momentarily cutting off all thought. But primarily, it is a continuous settling into the sky itself, to where there is no separation. We open ourselves to the entirety of the sky, fully utilizing our peripheral vision, until there is only gazing. We open to all of the sounds until they are a continuous symphony whose wash of sound is beyond any

single element. Immersed in our bodies, we feel the surface upon which we lie, we feel the weight of our bodies, not separate from the earth. Fully aware of all of these sensations, all of these sounds, all of these sights, we lie there gazing with the entirety of our being.

A shift occurs, where no longer are we gazing out into the sky, but it is as if the sky is gazing into us. This shift of perspective is the diminishing of the self, receding such that the filters the self places upon our senses no longer create that artificial separation. Persisting with this, even the subtle sense of separation, that is the feeling of the sky pressing down upon us, fades. Very gently, naturally, the self erodes; the barriers evaporate.

All that remains is empty awareness, not knowing whether eyes are open or closed, between earth and sky.

Tree Gazing

The entangled complexity of stands of trees, the branches of trees, networks of leaves can open us to awareness. When we encounter a tree with bare skeletal branches stark against the sky, or with a matrix of leaves and negative space, we stop and spend time gazing into them. We scan the branches, gazing into the negative space, letting patterns go. We let ourselves settle into just taking in a broad swath of the complex scene. Branches fray into fractal invisibility against blue or grey skies, pulling our gaze past ourselves. The network of negative space between leaves or branches, pulls us into connections away from our narratives.

This process requires time, especially as we first begin this practice. When we stop to gaze into a tree, it is not a matter of a glance upward and then moving on. We let our gaze caress the branches, lingering in gaps, roaming their extents, seamlessly transitioning to a wide open gaze, utilizing peripheral vision, and taking in the entire canopy, open to the interplay of negative space. When engaged in this practice while walking, we stop frequently and spend time with each suitable tree. As time passes, we find our thoughts less scattered and the narrative more distant, less urgent.

Over the course of dedicated periods of time, on a walk, or sitting and gazing into the entangled web-work of branches, leaves, grasses, shrubs or anything that creates complex fractal and negative spaces, we cultivate openness. With practice, we can spend most of this time just gazing, our mind a still pool, reflecting what it encounters, not casting our self into the world, but seamless with it, illuminated by it.

Mountain Gazing

There is no place for the self to find purchase amongst the mountains. The physicality of going deep into mountains roots us in our bodies, pushing us past our small concerns. Life and death have an immediacy that can be missed in the village. Surrounded by peaks, our selves are overwhelmed and thus reduced. Amidst towering indifference, we can let our selves completely go. Sitting amongst peaks, the artificiality of time as a construct reveals itself.

We sit amongst mountains and gaze at the range before us, dispensing with all names, labels, commentary or distinctions. The inner dialog naturally grows silent. We are simply still and allow the landscape to shine inward. Using our peripheral vision, we take in the full extent of the visible range. We notice any tension and place our awareness there, allowing it to ease. We let our eyes relax and unfocus or mostly close. We are with the mountains; there is no distinction between inside and outside, the gazer and what is gazed upon, sitter and mountain.

Eyes roam the edges of peaks, lingering on little spaces and gaps in the range. A waterfall pours down a crevasse, a pale thread though grays, greens, and browns. We perceive washes of colors as our gaze flows down the mountainside to the rocky valleys and green foothills, mountains beyond mountains, blue fading into distant peaks.

We gaze out toward a sawtooth ridge-line, forgetting ourselves in the infinite detail of the fractal edge; we experience ourselves from the mountain's perspective—a minute entity, not separate from any other, seamless with the surroundings. Eyes open, snapped into focus, there is no distinction.

Gazing Into the Distance

When we gaze across an open space—a pond, the ocean, a field, a lake, tundra, farmland ice sheets—into the distance, our perspective shifts. The sense of self begins to fade. When gazing into this wide immensity, utilizing our peripheral vision, this becomes ever more embodied.

We gaze long at the horizon, at the sawtooth of a distant mountain range or the fractal edge of a far away tree line. We roam our eyes across these features as the sense of isolated, separateness diminishes. Then we open up to the totality of the vast landscape in our gaze. Listening to sounds from far away enhances this sense of vast openness. We allow this complexity, this immensity to pervade our being. As with all of the gazing practices, this requires time.

When we gaze over a vast landscape, the shadows of clouds drift across the tableau. Following the contours of the scene, these shadows overlap, merge and intersect with other shadows, revealing boundless connections and, as they seamlessly merge without obstruction, interpenetration. We watch, open to the endless transformations, open to *reality as is*, no distinction between self and other.

When the sense of self is at a low ebb, we can invert our gaze, so that our perspective is that of the distant landscape shining into us. Instead of isolated bodies standing on the shore, or sitting overlooking a valley gazing outward, it is the mountains, plains, forest, or ocean gazing into us. Perception is identity and thus there is no distinction between gazing outwards and the outwards gazing inward. With continued practice, even this identity diminishes, the self unable to find purchase anywhere.

Gazing out toward distant rain clouds offers a similar evaporation of the diminished self. We gaze out at these clouds with their streaked, grey fingers of rain connecting earth to sky and fray into the cloud's perspective. Not only do we hover over a vast area, but we seamlessly connect to the landscape via countless drops of rain.

Entirely open to the totality of *what is*.

Listening

We gaze not just with our eyes but with our entire bodies. In the same way that we take in visual stimuli, in an all-at-once, diffused way, we listen to the totality of sounds.

We become still, open to our surroundings, our eyes fully relaxed, whether closed or slightly open. We let the sounds come in naturally, not straining to hear, not focusing on a particular sound, as if the sounds come from far away. The totality of the sounds form a singular soundscape, increasingly just a wash of sound.

When a sound draws our attention to it, we don't name it, comment upon it, tell a story about it, or dwell upon it. We simply are aware of that moment of focus and return to an open, expansive listening.

Undifferentiated sounds can lead us to a place of increasing openness, too expansive for our conceptual minds to grasp. The complexity of the sound-field is too much for our minds to take in, in its totality.

Rain falling on water, wind in the trees, the roar of ocean waves, the soft hiss of falling snow—these bring us to that diffused awareness.

But we do not depend upon any specific sounds, as the wash of sound is always present. We simply relax our listening and take it all in. The symphony of birds, insects, cars, planes, rustling grasses, falling leaves, all the myriad sounds are taken in all-at-once until all of the senses merge. As our focus relaxes, there is less reaching for labels, less conceptualization, and correspondingly, an increasing stillness. Even this stillness transforms, becoming less of something we can objectify, and becoming ever more present. It is this silence in which resides infinite potential—the space and energy for transformation.

When gazing with the eyes, we reach a place where we open further by listening. When walking, as we stop and gaze at various subjects, we open ourselves in a deeper way by opening to the sound field. When engaging in listening directly, we reach a place where visual sensation pours in. Indeed, we open up to all of our sensory experience: the wind on our skin, the taste of the air, the source where thoughts come from. We are truly open to the entirety of our experience, to what underlies experience, to *what is*.

The Night Sky

The strewn of stars in the night sky recenters our perspective, from the self toward totality. We operate from a false center, the sense that we are separate, an isolated individual moving through the world. The seeming infinity of the universe of stars undercuts that orientation.

We lay ourselves down, gazing directly up into the night sky. We gaze with our whole vision, sometimes roaming among the expanse, at other times, with our peripheral vision taking it in all-at-once. We ignore the mind's attempts to find patterns, to name things, to create that artificial distance. There are only the myriad stars gazing down into us.

Passing clouds, airplanes, shooting stars, birds, satellites–these amble across our field of view just as they are. We don't shift our attention in such a way as to create divisions. We don't resort to naming.

We further open ourselves by listening to the night sounds–the chirping of crickets, the creaking of trees, the wind in the grass, the scurrying of small animals, the hooting of owls, the nearly inaudible flapping of bat wings. Sounds seem magnified in the night, as we strain to recognize distant or faint sounds. It is a valuable practice to take them in without focusing on individual sounds, without labeling them. Open to sounds and the expanse above, there is only the earth and the sky, no separation.

The night sky with all its diversity—clouds, interconnected stars, planets, auroras—overwhelms us with its immensity and we can shift our perspective from the artificial center we have created and ultimately, let the self go and simply be.

Transformations

The setting and rising of the sun is an opportunity for gazing directly into impermanence. Sky-gazing into the distance, the setting sun shifts from yellow to red, painting the sky and any clouds with endless shades in between. The eye roams over clouds, over the long shadows, objects darkening and transforming in the shifting light. Sunset is a time for letting go, for seeing the transitory nature of all things directly. As light gradually fades away, stars poke out and we transition into gazing into the night sky, pinned to earth by the compound eye of uncountable stars.

When we watch things transform, day into night, or night into day, we are directly engaging with the myriad connections that are reality. The clouds, painted so dramatically, shift moment by moment. It is easy not to hold onto any single moment, as each successive moment is just as captivating. Attentively, we stay with this roiling flux, not grasping, not desiring, simply with *what is*.

Moon Gazing

When the moon is full, moonrise occurs as the sun sets. Transitioning from gazing at the sunset, we turn to the east and open to the moonrise. Yellow with reflected sunlight and, though a trick of the eye, deceptively large, moonrise allows us to put the self into perspective.

When the moon is at or near full, the quality of light and shadow is transformed. Gazing out at trees, into the distance, or at the night sky, they are transformed in unexpected and wondrous ways. Walking under the full moon, we walk from the abdomen, our center of gravity. Our gaze wide, open to what is really going on. It is the same, yet different, from walking in daylight and it is this difference that highlights the shift in perspective. This is a window into the arbitrariness of our views and an invitation to increased flexibility. All the myriad perspectives are a site of practice.

Sailing through wind-torn clouds, an absence in the deep blue sky, a shining beacon in pitch dark skies, the faintest sliver like a shifted disc revealing the light behind, the moon draws our gaze in all its manifestations: the nail-paring-thin moon at dawn, the half moon in daylight blue sky, the full moon illuminating the inky night with deep shadows. We sit and observe the moon, embracing its contours, letting the pure, clean bright flame of awareness shine into us.

We set out to see the moon, moon gazing as an activity, a practice. We find a moon gazing platform—a deck, a rock, a patch of grass, a hill, bluff or mountainside. There is the moon, nameless, simply itself. We let our gaze wander over its surface, the jagged edge of a crescent moon, the myriad features of the full moon, its interplay with clouds, stars, passing objects. The moon may inspire words, but we let those flow away, The moon shines into us, pins us down, lets us forget our sense of separation.

We lay back and let the moon illuminate us, the piercing light of awareness.

Gazing In Motion

Gazing at myriad objects in motion defies our singular casting of attention and opens us up to the complexity of natural processes. Sunlight dancing on the surface of water, flocks of birds, swarms of insects, falling snow, dust frolicking in a ray of light–all of these can bring us to openness.

If out walking, we move through space, letting sights and sounds pass through us, uncommented upon. At an opportune locale, we pause and gaze out into the distance. We gaze across a pond with our entire vision letting the play of ripples, flickering sunlight, gnats roiling in the air, trees swaying in the wind, or whatever is present simply be in our field of vision. We avoid directing attention toward any singular object. If a bird or insect flies across our field of view, we just let them fly by. These transitory events come into sight, persist for a time and then pass outside of our view.

As our minds begin to reflect the view shining in and the narrative is at a low ebb, we remain with the awareness of the transitory passage of a bird. It is impossible to hold in our mind, but we remain aware of it as it passes beyond our field of view. Following the birds, without looking at them, we shift to their viewpoint. We see the fields that they fly across from above, the shifting colors and details of the terrain. We open our gaze to the shifting seas below, slate gray upon gray, restless in motion.

We open our awareness to the paths and views of multiple birds as they fly by. Opening ourselves up to them, we move with them, as them, hopping from branch to branch, wheeling above the ocean, darting across the sky. None of this is beyond awareness. The infinite interconnections of totality belie any distinction, all phenomena interpenetrating. We are the flying birds, the swarming insects, the child running along the seashore, the car driving on the road, the sunbeams dancing on the water.

We open to the swirling complexity of the background and the ceaseless movement of the foreground, we let go of that distinction, let go of all divisions and what remains is the infinite interplay of *reality as is*.

Fire Gazing

Fire is constant transformation, it is impermanence in action. We gaze into the dancing flames, endlessly shaded coals, charred wood, and layered ash. Wood transforms into ash and gazing into the fire, we can see the myriad stages of change all at once.

Beyond this, gazing into the flames, into the glowing heart of the coals, here we see an endless weaving beyond our comprehension. Gazing into this patternless formation, letting go of our attempt to force it into shape, to make sense of what is essentially ungraspable, the sense of separation diminishes. There is only the flames, only the glowing furnace in the heart of the wood.

We hear the crackling of the burning wood, sudden pops as some pitch, or moisture suddenly evaporates, the background roaring of the displacement of air, the hissing of sparks rising into the night sky. Open to the dancing flames, open to the diversity of sounds, we feel the heat radiating outward. We feel it on our skin. We gaze into fire with our entire bodies, tasting the ash, feeling the heat, and smelling the smoke. When we open to all our senses, there is only awareness.

In the act of gazing into that which is inherently unknowable, the grasping mind can find no purchase. Then we are open to transformation, beyond lack of separation, experiencing constant flux and seeing into its nature. As we open up completely, we drop the sense of permanence of a lasting, unchanging self and there is only connection, only change, everything interpenetrating.

Gazing Into Water

Water in all its multiplicity of forms reveals the ever-changing nature of all phenomena and by gazing deeply into it, we open to this essential truth. Water can be a mirror, a literal manifestation of the still pool. When we gaze into it in this form, the myriad reflections—the clarity of the water, the depths below, the ground beneath—all intermingle beyond graspability. An insect striding across the surface breaks up this layer, distorts the reflections and leaves us with little to hold onto. Wind just stirring the water generates endless abstractions, subverting the mind of representation, the mind that divides, that categorizes and names. As the wind grows ever stronger ripples, little waves weave endless patterns that confound categorization, leaving the discriminating mind with scant to work with. Sunlight bouncing off of ripples dances endlessly, unpredictably, chaotically eluding our desire for regularity, pattern and stasis.

In all these forms and endless others, water provides one of the richest and adaptable subjects for gazing. It can reflect the clouds and negative space for sky gazing, but stirring it around, inverting it, undermining our expectations, and revealing interpenetration. Trees reflected in the water, layered with each other, fragmented by movement, subverts our desire for patterns, eliding our grasp. When a single drop of rain falls into this watery mirror, it shatters our views. When gazing into water's reflective nature, we take in all the layers as a whole—the muddy bottom, the watery layers, the glassy surface and all the mirrored phenomena: rocks, trees, sky, and mountains. The interpenetration of phenomena is on display. We simply allow disturbances in the water to bring home the contingent nature of all things. We let the reflections shine into us and we are as a mirror to them.

We can sit and gaze across water, watching the ripples weave endless configurations, patterns that are beyond our kin. We gaze with relaxed eyes, utilizing the full breadth of our vision. The patterns simply come in and we cannot conceptually categorize them; beyond words, beyond understanding.

Falling water is constantly in motion, it is endlessly transforming, manifesting in countless ways. We take it all in, making no attempt to find patterns, to grasp at any feature, to lose ourselves in the spray, rainbows, arcs, or cascades. We gaze across the constantly agitated pool, letting the pattern of infinity play across our mind, not desiring anything, just letting what is happening occur. There is falling water, echoing the rise and fall of thoughts, of lives, of totality.

When there are ripples in the water and sunlight

shining on them, it is broken into spots, seeming to dance across the water like a natural display of static. Truly random, it defies our mind's attempts at prediction, at forcing the display into a pattern. Completely beyond our control, this makes for one of the most powerful subjects for gazing, as there is literally nothing to cling to. As the waves shift, the sun moves in the sky, the wind changes, the dancing light becomes more or less active, and more or less distributed across our view. Again we want to take in the whole scene: the patterns of the water, the patterns of the light, any reflections, just let the entirety of this overwhelming sensory experience shine in.

We gaze across a lake, in its stillness, at the trees on the far side, and at the reflections softly distorting in the water. We gaze across the ocean with its endless waves, at the fuzzy line of the horizon. We can watch waves roll in and out leaving intricate patterns of foam, tracing incomprehensible symbols in the sand.

In all cases, we open ourselves up to the weave of the water, its endless complexity, and constant change. Our minds, unable to separate and grasp this, have to just let it go. We let the small self recede into the waves, lost in the bottomless reflections, fading away like the momentary twinkle of the setting sun on unsettled water.

Walking

We walk with full awareness of the body, from the body. We facilitate this if necessary by placing attention on the abdomen, being aware of the rise and fall of breath. We walk from this center of gravity, simply letting sights and sounds flow through. Periodically, we stop, direct our gaze to our breath, and exhale. We pause for a moment, letting go. We direct our gaze to distant things such as the sky, mountain ranges, tree-lines, and edges of buildings. We resume walking after a moment and maintain just an embodied sense of awareness, walking from the abdomen. We shift awareness to the abdomen as thoughts arise, but then open it up to our entire body and beyond. All sensations, sights, sounds, feelings, and scents come in without placing our direct gaze upon them. We do not name them, comment upon them, or distinguish them.

When gazing at phenomena, we look for complexity with contrast, something beyond what attention can contain. The contrast is essential, as an undifferentiated mass doesn't allow for flow from the singular to seamlessness. Thin branches, like a tangle of veins contrasted with a piercing blue sky, is a concrete example. We can only take it in all-at-once, but it isn't merely a wash of color. At all times, avoid categorizing or naming what arises in our gaze, or providing a commentary to the unfolding of experience. We avoid criticizing ourselves. If we find ourselves slipping into a narrative, we simply note this without critique and return to walking, directing attention to the abdomen.

As we work with this practice, and remember that all of these practices require time, we will find ourselves increasingly open, with fewer thoughts bubbling up. Those thoughts that do arise simply pour away. This leads to the most natural form of walking where instead of projecting our self out into the world, the world shines in on us. This is the condition of walking without separation, without distinction of self and other, simply moving through the world without obstruction. Empty awareness.

We walk out in the woods, across fields, in mountains, on the beach, in the landscape. As we walk, our gaze takes in what comes, all the forms shining within. We walk in our bodies, from the abdomen, breathing naturally. We pause and gaze out in the distance. If birds fly across our gaze, we hold them in our minds, no separation. If the tops of the trees sway, they sway in our minds. Sunlight dances on water, dragonflies dart through our field of view. We let all of these reflect in the deep still pool of our minds.

We stop, let out a breath and gaze out at anything, any layered complexity, negative space, or distant fractal landscape. Our thoughts pour away until there is only empty awareness. We return to walking, remaining in that modality. When our attention is caught, we notice this and direct it to our center of gravity. Keeping our attention on the abdomen, we feel our breath, the diaphragm sinking to its natural extent. We are simply walking in emptiness. Simply walking.

Investigation

Investigation

Sit quietly, completely relaxed and engaged, cultivating the still pool. A stillness arises; we are only in our bodies, not seeking elsewhere. Thoughts are not pursued nor cut off. Our baseline feeling is one of equanimity. When even that sense of sitting recedes, we reside in openness, from which we are able to investigate the self.

There are numerous methods of investigation that we engage with: investigating thoughts, probing, interrogation and, most fundamentally, the sense of uncertainty itself. The process of investigation is to work through the supports that prop up the self: thoughts, conditioning, memories, feelings and other ad hoc structures that we mistakenly identify as who we truly are. This is a process of directly shaking loose our conditioning.

Following on naturally from cultivating openness, we investigate thoughts by observing them as they rise and fall away. These thoughts—where do they come from and where do they go? In the course of investigation, we come to see thoughts as just another sense, not separate from us, but not who we really are.

The various methods of questioning can stir up

buried memories, painful experiences, social conditioning, and long repressed feelings. We use the process of letting go to work through these attachments. Questioning allows us to recognize them, to surface them, and to name them. Letting go is how we discover, integrate and finally loosen their grip upon us until they no longer have any purchase.

Probing is particularly amenable to fundamental questions of the form, "*who am I*"? These are questions that examine our provisional selves and the conditioning that supports it. We continue to question any answers that surface and thus, this is an extremely useful tool for practicing without guidance. There is no bottom to the questioning. There is no endpoint, no point where we can say "*I am done.*"

Interrogation is particularly effective in working with contradiction and questions of what remains. In the course of practice, we see through the self in an initial breakthrough and because our conditioning is so strong, we need to continue practicing, to continue questioning. This is particularly where questions of "*what remains*" come into play. "*What remains*" is where we question our assumptions of who we are, of what constitutes reality. "*If we are not those things, if those things aren't fundamental aspects of reality, then what is?*" These questions will invariably be individual to the practitioner but there are general forms that are used widely. This is the case where a Good Friend can be helpful, providing the questions that we, operating from our own conditioning, may not have chosen.

Probing and interrogation work together hand in hand. Truly, any question can be investigated with either method. We may probe in the course of daily life but in periods of intense practice, we interrogate. In this way, our investigation is always ongoing, continuing on in all aspects of our lives.

The nature of investigation is to find out who we truly are, to encounter that which is real. In the course of investigation, what we have always taken as our identity, as what is real, is constantly found to be insufficient, not the whole truth. This is the great uncertainty, that unease that arises as what we have taken to be true is undermined. We deliberately cultivate this uncertainty, relentlessly questioning our assumptions, constantly rejecting theories, conceptualizations and answers. This sense of uncertainty becomes our entire focus until it finally collapses, leaving us face to face with *reality as is*.

Investigating Thoughts

In essence, there is no inside or outside. This notion inherently fosters a sense of separateness. With all of our senses, whether it be sight, sound, smell, taste, touch or thought, we can directly perceive the source. Gazing fosters openness, but also allows us to see subtle processes of separation. All of the methods we engage in synergistically work together as approaches toward openness, and close observation of these hinge points of separation.

When we turn our gaze inward and engage in close observation of thought, we are led to the source. We observe our thoughts without effort, allowing them to rise and fall away. We do not try to cut them off. We do not try to suppress them. Exerting any form of control reinforces the self, concretizes that sense of a separate entity that tries to exert this control. We are simply aware of our thoughts and this alone allows them to naturally fade away. The nature of thought is to arise and then fade into nothingness. As we simply allow this process to unfold, the thoughts slow down. We notice when we chase after a thought, when we turn it into a narrative, and this very act of noticing causes these thoughts to die away.

As we become adroit at simply being with our thoughts, they settle, and in those deepening moments between thoughts, there is genuine stillness. We see that we are not these thoughts, that they are another sense that we make use of, and are impermanent, transitory events with no abiding essence. In this stillness, we are aware of where the thoughts arise from, and where they fade into. In this openness, there is endless potential.

This is a nodal point, where through the cultivation of the still pool, the ever expansive openness of gazing from eyes or ears and the relentless probing of investigation all converge. We see that the self is not any of these things and we question, *"what is it?"*

Our investigations begin in this stillness., in no longer identifying with thought, and in putting down the separateness inherent in looking and hearing. In this dynamic openness, we are simply engaged with *what is.*

When we no longer identify with thoughts, we can see that they are no different from any other sensation. They are part of our experience, not separate or outside. Indeed in each thought, there is totality.

Probing

There are fundamental questions of the self that we can ask, dropping them like a pebble into the still pool and waiting to see what the ripples bring to the shore. This method, of fully cultivating the still pool and asking questions and then seeing what arises, is a powerful mode of investigation. Our minds will bring up many things in this process, some banal, some demanding further inquiry.

The fundamental questions that we ask ourselves are varied and everyone will have their own individual approach to them. But the core questions are all variants on two essential questions: *"who am I"*? and *"what is it"*?, which are themselves two expressions of the one truth.

These questions can be expressed as:

—*"Who am I?"*
—*"What is true?"*
—*"Who is listening?"*
—*"What is real?"*
—*"What am I?"*
—*"What is this?"*

Taking these core questions and modifying them to our immediate circumstances can be an effective approach for every practitioner.

Indirect Probing

With indirect probing, we load our minds with the question and let it be worked on in our subconscious. Throughout the day, we may ask the question to keep it active, but the process is more background. Our subconscious strives to solve the question, just as we may wake up from sleep with the answer to a problem from our daily activities. With these questions having no answer, the contradiction generates increasing uncertainty, ultimately confounding the conceptual mind. Over time the conceptual mind begins to break down, revealing its constructed and illusory nature. If at times an answer seems to arise, perhaps on waking, perhaps in a flash of intuition, then we question that. Any answer becomes our next question until there are no questions left, the self falling away.

Direct Probing

With direct probing, we also occupy the conceptual mind with the question, periodically asking it throughout the day. But during times where we are able to engage in dedicated practice—stillness-sitting, walking and other periods devoted to contemplation—we inquire directly. We calm our thoughts, cultivating the still pool, then we ask the question. Whatever may bubble up—notions of identity, social conditioning, biological constructs, archetypal figures, deep conditioning—we also question. We continue to question any sort of "answer." Ultimately, these answers are the supports we have constructed for our sense of a separate self and through investigation, we reveal that there is nothing there. This process is not one of invoking the will; it is simply asking a question and waiting in openness. At times, responses can come fast and when they do, we simply continue to question them, like a child who always asks, "why," to any given explanation. At other times, we can simply settle into the still pool, open and resonating with *what is*.

These two modes of probing can, of course, work in concert. Throughout the day, regardless of the activity we are engaged in, we keep the question alive in our minds. It is the first thing we think of in the morning, and the last at night. In any space in our day, we can delve deeper, questioning any response, investigating "*who am I?*," "*what is this?*"

Interrogation

A primary tool of investigation is to set our gaze directly upon the subject and engage in intense questioning. In this method, we follow the basic procedure for all of these practices: we relax into the still pool, and focus on the breath. Once calm, we shift our focus from the breath to the question. We ask ourselves the question with a sincere spirit of not knowing. It is the not-knowing, this sense of questioning, that is essential. We ask ourselves the question and remain in that modality of questioning. If thoughts arise, or we shift away from questioning, we ask the question again. Our focus is only on the question and a deep sense of uncertainty, of not-knowing. These questions that we ask, of the fundamental nature of reality, we cannot conceive of in a conceptual way. The only way to resolve these questions is to bypass the separate self and resolve it in our original nature.

When gazing at the question, there is nothing else that our awareness settles on. The questioning is not aligned with the breath; our bodies fall away in the course of the questioning. The questioning can become intense, which can be felt as the mind being tense, and this is an aspect of the process. However if we find our bodies becoming tense, we shift aware-ness to the body and engage with the relaxation process.

It is not the case of asking the question repeatedly like a mantra; it is not the case of using it to cut off thoughts; it is not the case that the question becomes an object; it is not the case that we identify with the question; it is not the case that there is a conceptual "answer" to the question. These are all pitfalls to be vigorously avoided. We resist these tendencies by noticing that we are falling into them and then just asking the question again. The essence is the sense of uncertainty, the not-knowing and that develops through persistent asking of the question and staying with the uncertainty, no matter how overwhelming it may become.

The sense of not-knowing can become physical, like that bottomless sinking sensation in our stomach when we are anxious. This sense of not-knowing will grow until we feel an overwhelming sense of appre-hension and uncertainty. We don't know the answer but the most important thing, the only thing, is to resolve the question. We must know. It will become increasingly overwhelming until suddenly, at the op-portune moment, it collapses and we experience reali-ty directly, as is.

The initial question that we must resolve is that of,

"*what is this?*" This is the question of emptiness, of connections, of the nature of reality. We use the process to ask ourselves, "*what is this*," or directly inquire into emptiness with that questioning spirit. This is the fundamental questioning into *reality as is*. This question is one that has no bottom, that one can explore from breakthrough to breakthrough and thus can be pursued throughout all the modalities of practice.

As the conceptual mind breaks down, we are constantly faced with what remains. If what our conceptual minds construct isn't true and we put it down, then what remains? Constantly we are forced to turn away from what we feel should be and are faced with *what is*. Never trying to answer, we simply keep asking the question, which contradicts any answer that we may come up with.

Relentlessly asking the question whenever conceptualizations arise, there is no space for our tendency to divide into this and that. We see the contradiction of the dualities we encounter, the contradiction that is our separateness. Never taking "yes" for an answer, we interrogate deeper and deeper until all understandings, all conceptual supports and sense of self are put down. What remains?

Contradiction

Because all things arise from the web of totality that is *reality as is*, our experience is rife with contradictions. *This* and *that* are simultaneously *not-this* and *not-that* and bear no fundamental separation. Things seemingly in opposition can be both a reflection of experiential reality being dependent upon circumstances or, by considering each thing individually, present us with a wider perspective. We can be asked to examine something from one view as fundamental reality and then examine its opposite as just another aspect of experiential reality. For where can anything arise but from the connections of *reality as is*? All of the dualities, contradictory thoughts, and paradoxical views—all are contained within totality.

Engaging directly with contradiction is a way to get past our discriminating, conceptual mind. Deeply grappling with an object—a word, a statement, a core question—and following it down to its essential emptiness is a path to insight. Then contemplating its opposite to the same place can open us to yet a deeper insight. Working with contradictory statements can efficiently reveal this inherent emptiness, that ultimately there is no there, there.

The method of working with contradiction is in

utilizing questions, prompts, and dialogs, that elide conceptualization, that have no "answer" or "solution" that can be puzzled out, or arrived at by thinking. This is the inherent nature of contradiction: to resolve the contradiction we have, to abandon critical processes, and let go of conceptualization.

As we simply observe these things, observe without seeking, we can see where one transforms into the other. It is at that point of transformation that things are the most uncertain. Close observation of these interstices, free of conceptualization, free of will, and free of effort, generates bewildering uncertainty, building up to a great mass as we gaze ever closer into the morass until finally, we just let it go.

There is an inherent contradiction in all our senses, in that division into self and other. Looking out in the world, there is the division of inside and outside, the gazer and the gazed-upon. If we apply this same methodology, we can see where this transforms and push ourselves to remain at this boundary point until it dissolves. Likewise, with the hearer and the heard, the thinker and the thought, the subject and the object. When we don't dwell in these dualities, when we see from the One Mind, there is no coming or going. Motion is stillness. Stillness is motion. We dwell nowhere, fully alert and truly free.

Encounter

When we encounter a good friend, there is an immediate recognition and we acknowledge this, asking *"how are you?"* This is an invitation to allow original nature to flow through us. If the initial serve isn't answered, we don't force it. We smile and nod and move on. But when a good friend takes up the challenge, then the game is afoot.

We respond with immediacy, fully engaged in the encounter. If we hesitate, we are lost and a good friend will end the encounter abruptly. When we respond without hesitation the ball moves to our friend's side of the court. They too respond with immediacy. In this way, good friends constantly press each other, unmovable in continuous practice.

Students of *reality as is* who are well down the path can arrange for encounters in a formal way with those of training. Not swayed by the back and forth volleying of the encounter, they remain unmoved, holding serve. In the course of encounter, they present questions and weigh the response, plumbing the depths of our understanding, and calling us out when the conceptual mind reasserts itself. They can, in the midst of the demanding process of interrogation, navigate their way through contradiction, and clearly see what remains. During a period of intensive practice, we can consistently meet every day, and be constantly pushed harder and further.

Without the rigor and testing of encounter, we are too easily fooled by our small selves, too easily satisfied with limited insights, too willing to feel we have gone far enough, to think we are "done," and to be caught in our egos. A good friend calls us out when we succumb to these tricks of the self, keeping us on the path, pushing us further.

As we move along the way, we are all called upon to be a good friend, to engage in these encounters. This is a path of constant investigation, continuous practice and uncompromising interrogation.

Deeper Investigation

When we investigate with genuine commitment, relentlessly staying with the question until the self falls away, this is not the end of the investigation. It is at that point—when the self collapses, we encounter *reality as is,* and we engage in direct unmediated experience—that we have truly begun. The experience of no-self is not one that can be described. One who has only known the self cannot imagine it. When it occurs, we will know it and we will know that all the other experiences that we have in the course of practice are just that: experiences.

The experience of total absorption, tranquility, bliss, ecstasy, I-am-everything, everything-is-me, and all-is-one, are all of the self. These can be wonderful states, powerful experiences and worth having, but they are not the self falling away. This is important to understand before we move on from the core investigations previously described. If there is any doubt, we just continue with the investigation as we have been doing. None of these questions have any bottom and we can always probe deeper.

When the self does fall away, we can see all of our experiences for what they are. There is a period of time when we operate without the filter of the self, responding to circumstances naturally, and without obstruction. But we have simply bypassed all of our conditioning in the course of dropping the self. Our conditioning is memories, tied in with a sense of self and emotion, and these will cause the self to reform. We are more aware of its constructed nature, more aware of our conditioning, and more easily able to let go. It is at this point that we engage in deeper investigation.

Probing Deeper

The most essential question that we use for probing is, "*who am I?*" When we have resolved this question, through the dropping away of the self, then we continue our investigation, probing from all angles:
—"*What am I?*"
—"*Where am I?*"
—"*Why am I?*"
These alternate views will continue to shake loose the fetters of the self, revealing the beliefs, the fears, and the conditioning that supports and ultimately constitutes the self. We probe deep into these questions and all the questions they stir up. We begin to reveal questions that are directly tied to our conditioning. We probe into those. The deepest forms of probing into the self are questions that are individual to us, highly specific and formed from our own con-

ditioning.

Deeper Interrogation

When we shatter the uncertainty that we have generated with our interrogation into *"what is this,"* or investigating what remains there is no doubt that the self has been put down. The uncertainty beforehand is like a great block obscuring everything, yet we still function. It is unmistakable when that is broken through. But the self, supported by a lifetime of conditioning, will reconstitute itself. There are many questions of a contradictory nature that we can utilize to continue the process. These questions must attract the self, yet confound it. At times, a good friend will provide us a question that has no resonance, that perhaps even repels us. That may be just what is needed at that moment. If we are working with a good friend, follow their lead.

These questions that confound us, stripped of all of their trappings, resolve to this question:

"Nothing you do will do, so what do you do?"

No response we give suffices, so how do we respond? Interrogate this thoroughly. We gaze at it without ceasing, giving it all of our energy. Nothing will do. Exhaust all conceptualization. Every answer, every response we give is answered with, *"that won't do, so what do you do?"* The uncertainty grows ever greater.

Bring it to encounter if working with a good friend who has seen through this question. In periods of intensive practice, we give ourselves completely to the question, interrogating with abandon until this too shatters.

Opening to Uncertainty

As we relentlessly interrogate, an overwhelming sense of uncertainty arises, a deep, penetrating not-knowing. All of our doubts, all of our feelings, all of our underlying conditioning can be pushed into this uncertainty. As our familiarity with this practice grows, the uncertainty becomes another companion, a sensation that we do not necessarily need to arouse by words. The most fundamental question, the question of existence that bedevils all of us, is *"where did we come from and where do we go?"* These questions of life and death are at the root of all our fears, all our conditioning, and all questions lead to it. This is the question we must resolve and we must answer it for ourselves, or that sense of unease that haunts our lives will never cease. Not-knowing is the essence of this matter and through deep investigation, we develop that great blocking uncertainty.

This all pervasive not-knowing is fundamentally the same place that we arrive at when we are truly non-dwelling. There is nowhere to rest, nothing to hold onto, only *reality as is*, which is beyond our grasp. Utter not-knowing. Opening to totality brings us to this place of non-dwelling. When we cultivate the still pool, our baseline feeling is one of equanimity. This is a place where we are increasingly open and flexible with whatever arises. Putting down everything we can hold onto; this is truly non-dwelling. If we shift our baseline feeling from one of equanimity to one of not-knowing, then great uncertainty develops. We can, in expansive openness, give rise to uncertainty by simply tapping into that sense of dis-ease. If needed, we familiarize ourselves with it by asking ourselves, *"what is death?" "Where did we come from?" "What happens after we die?"* These questions will arouse that sense of dis-ease, of anxiety, that is always with us. It then becomes straightforward to simply rouse that feeling and shift our baseline. Dwelling nowhere, open to *what is*, with nothing to hold onto, eventually the uncertainty expands until it becomes blocking, until it overwhelms and collapses and only *what is* remains.

Continuous
Practice

Single-Tasking

In our ordinary activities, we are always engaged with practice when we are single-tasking. When we take part in any activity, we are just doing that activity. When we walk, we are walking; when we are eating, we are eating; when we are sitting, we are sitting. We are open to all that is around us, but we keep our focus on the activity at hand.

Our tendency, instead of being engaged with what is really going on, is to be lost in our thoughts, feelings, and emotions. We dwell in the past, or daydream about the future, instead of being with what is happening right now. We go through this life reacting to these thoughts, feelings, and emotions, not seeing them for what they are: as things that arise, persist for some time, then fall away. Much of what we do in the practice is to learn to see thoughts as just thoughts, not as who we are. Practicing single-tasking in all our endeavors helps us to stay with *what is*, not with transitory experiences.

We can utilize many of the practices outlined here to bring us back in line with what is really going on. When walking from place to place, we keep our awareness on our abdomen, open to our surroundings. When eating, we keep our awareness on the sensation of taste, fully absorbed in the taste of our food and drink. If we are listening to natural sounds or looking at scenery, there are just the sounds, just the scenery. We aren't losing ourselves in thoughts about how we will tell others about them, write about them, or any other way of mediating the experience. There is just the experience as it is happening. Beyond engaging with what is happening with attentiveness, we will find all of these sensations and experiences far more rewarding when single-tasking. As we stay with a single experience, it becomes dominant with all of its features and nuances, and our experiences become filled with wonder and we take delight in every action.

As we move beyond sensations to all of our activities, we find they are all enriched in just this way. When in a conversation, simply listen completely, only hearing what the other person is saying. Listening in this way, we find that we are far more attuned to the other person, and far more able to actually communicate. In a meeting, we may find we are the only one actually present, actually engaged with what is happening. Tasks we engage in, like cooking, cleaning, writing, and repairing things all are the most important thing in this moment and that manifests in the results. Even when we find we have to manage multiple things at once, we give each thing our full attention as we move between them.

Our natural way of engaging in the world is one of single-tasking. We are present, engaged, attentive. We respond with naturalness, equanimity and flexibility. We are not pushed around by our thoughts, feelings and emotions. We are able to see them for what they are, feel them fully and let them go. Our way is one of moving through this world without obstruction and single-tasking is an essential aspect actualizing this.

Solitude

The practice of solitude is one of letting go. Giving up on comfort, distractions, society, entertainment, and civilization itself. To withdraw for a time—and it must only be for a time—is an essential endeavor for truly confronting *reality as is*. Much of what we attach to are left behind. Many of the routines we cling to—the security of family, friends, jobs, not to mention the structures and protections of society—are dispensed with. True solitude is a radical letting go. It is an opportunity to just be, to plumb the depths, and to sit and gaze at *what is*.

We leave behind distractions, comforts and entertainment. We take only what is necessary, and what facilitates complete engagement. We travel to where the surroundings can activate and feed our practice: mountains, oceans, forests, rivers, and deserts.

When engaging in the practice of solitude, it is essential that we develop, and adheres to, a routine. Otherwise, it is easy to fall out of practice, to fall into distraction or dullness. Extended periods of solitude that are devoid of practice lead to despair. We set a routine where we mix physical activities, stillness-sitting, walking, and engaged work throughout the day. We take care of our surroundings attentively. We take care of our body attentively.

We start each day with engaged movements: slow, contemplative, and grounded in the body. Then, we follow this with a period of stillness-sitting. Depending on the circumstances, this could be outdoors, watching the sun rise, or sitting in the dark in whatever structure we find ourselves. We sit for a prescribed amount of time. Single-tasking, we prepare our morning meal and eat, attentive to the actions of eating. Perhaps during the day, we clean our residence, being with the movement, the gesture of working. We take a walk, gazing at the features that present themselves. Creative endeavors can naturally fit into our routine like writing, painting, and playing music. When we are single-tasking, we are practicing; in solitude this comes naturally. In this way, we orient this period of solitude around practice. We mix stillness-sitting, gazing, and engaged activity into a seamless whole.

We can retreat into solitude temporally or for extended durations, as it is ultimately a state of being. If we can let go of the trappings of civilization for a day, a week, a year, or half a lifetime, it will bring us closer to *what is*. Solitude is not escape so always in the end, we return to face the challenges that circumstances present, to give ourselves to those in need.

Pilgrimage

Pilgrimage is intimately connected to solitude; it can be understood as searching for solitude. If the practice of solitude is one of letting go, the practice of pilgrimage is one of commitment. It is to commit to being fully engaged just with the practice for an extended duration. On pilgrimage, we only take what is necessary for the journey and we engage completely in the practice. Pilgrimage is not to travel to some place designated as exceptional or imbued with some sort of transcendent power. It is just this taking of our practice beyond our comfort zones, to where we can directly engage with natural processes. It is practice in motion.

Pilgrimage is a practice in which we engage with our entire being with solitude. Some pilgrimages are a continuous journey—often under our own power—in which we find solitude in motion. We practice on the journey, which takes us ever deeper into solitude.

Other pilgrimages are to places particularly amenable to engagement—a mountain, a hidden beach, or a secluded valley—a place of retreat where solitude can unfold naturally. Perhaps we find it in a cove on this wilderness beach, or a short bushwhack off the trail to a mountain overlook, or even in a tent at the end of a day of travel.

Pilgrimage, however we undertake it, demands, and is sustained, by a deep commitment to engage in the practice of all things.

We journey without goals, as an end in itself, not oriented toward some destination. In this way, pilgrimage mirrors the practice. It is the practice. There is practice; there is the journey, no distinction. There is nothing that is being gained, nothing that is being discarded. The journey is not undertaken to produce something, as with a job, or as a lifestyle. It is practice and undertaken with that orientation.

On pilgrimage, the practice is one of responding to circumstances. While we may spend time in solitude at various points where a predictable routine can be established, in the course of travel, the unexpected is a constant companion. We are able to practice equanimity, to respond to *what is* and not pursue what should be.

Likewise the opportunities for encounter are expanded and test our flexibility. We find on pilgrimage strangers will often confide in us, question us in probing ways, or confront us with unexpected situations. How we respond is a chance to plumb the depths. Do we respond with equanimity? Do we help where we can? Are we open enough to ask for help when we need it? We can discover on pilgrimage the erosion of our habitual responses and the upending of our routines. How we respond to circumstances is a constant source of practice.

In its most engaged form, the Dream Mountain Way is one of continual pilgrimage, always engaged in the practice, responding to circumstances as they come, always in motion, never dwelling anywhere.

Continuous Practice

The Dream Mountain Way is a pragmatic, hands-on approach to continuous practice. In our daily lives, on pilgrimage, in solitude, on retreat, amidst all activity—in every circumstance, everything is an opportunity for practice. We must strive to not limit ourselves to any particular modality. It is the circumstances that arise in every domain that we must respond to and that is the most essential practice. We take every opportunity, every moment, as a good friend, pointing at the way, illuminating where there is work to be done, endlessly murmuring *"not yet"*, *"not yet."*

We wake up in our bodies, staying with our sensations, and perform our morning routines with attentiveness. As we move from place to place, we stay with our bodies, our awareness on our center of gravity, our gaze wide. We move naturally through our environment. We cultivate openness as we move through our day, taking advantage of the circumstances that afford themselves. Elements of the landscape, moments in between tasks, all of our daily activities are opportunities for practice. We stay with our bodies and are fully present for whatever we are engaged in, single-tasking. Fully attentive to what we are doing, lively and responsive, all of our interactions are practice. When space allows, we open ourselves to our bodies, and our surroundings, aligning ourselves with *what is*.

When we spend time in stillness-sitting, we cultivate the still pool. We are present in our bodies, simply sitting, rooted in the earth, attentive to the rise and fall of our abdomens, and increasingly open. We watch our thoughts arise dispassionately, without chasing after them or cutting them off. We avoid commentary, criticism, and negative actions. Sights, sounds, and sensations are all present but are not labeled, described or dwelled upon. We stay attentive and do not get caught up in a story.

Probing into *what is,* we investigate questions that cut through our sense of a separate self, and our constructed identities. We delve into the essential questions of life and death, prying deeply into this matter. We fully integrate the question into all our activities. As we walk, work and sit throughout the day, we return to the question, raising it over and over into total awareness. We remain attentive to the task at hand, fully engaging with it, then return to the question. In stillness-sitting, we drop the question into the still pool. When out gazing, we drop the question into negative space. The question is the last thought we raise before sleep and the first thought in the morning.

Encounters throughout the day, all situations are an opportunity to practice, indeed they are the most opportune. For this is a practice of everyday life, the circumstances that we find ourselves in with all its entanglements, connections, vexations, beauty, joys and complexity. All circumstances are a teacher, showing us another view, another angle, giving us a new opportunity to respond. We strive to be in alignment with *what is*; in each and every moment, we are fully present, flexible, engaged, and ever more open.

Patterning

Naturalness

When we utilize the self to direct energy toward our actions, we will always be separated from them. We will operate a step removed from circumstances. When our energy flows effortlessly through us, it is directed toward what we are engaged in and we interact with circumstances naturally, without constructed barriers. This is our natural condition, not the mediation and distancing that the self forces upon what arises.

We truly have nothing to do; our natural condition is one of energy freely flowing through us to where it is required. This is a modality of immediacy, responding naturally with our entire being. When we are open to *what is*, we are an expression of it. We practice this in walking, gazing, in the still pool, and in every circumstance.

When stillness-sitting, every time we notice we are off our method and return to the method, we engage the self. We expend energy that could be directed toward engaging with *what is*. When we stay on method, we conserve our energy. To cultivate this, we do not waste energy in commentary, or self-criticism when we slip off-method. We do not make a big effort to stay on task. We simply shine the light of awareness on thoughts, on images, and on distractions. In this way, they automatically die away and we remain open. In time, we are just open and when thoughts arise, they fade away naturally. In the same way, we engage in all our gazing, our investigation, and in bringing practice to all our activities.

When investigating, it is particularly essential that the process of noticing when we are caught in distractions and raising the question occur with the minimum expenditure of energy. As the uncertainty grows, all our energy is poured into it. When we save energy by not needing to continuously raise the question, the uncertainty grows accordingly. We simply notice when distractions have taken over and raise the question. Soon, the felt sense of the question suffices, the words fade and there is just that sense when we find ourselves off-method. Naturally, we stay with uncertainty until we see through it.

Moving through the world without mediation, without the distancing narrative of the self, we can utilize self-direction as a tool, quickly discarding it once it sets in motion the process. As we become increasingly open, that separateness ebbs away and, in the midst of activity, there is no effort, no movement, no resistance, and no doing.

Flexibility

As we naturally move through this world, circumstances will arise and we respond directly and supplely. When it is incumbent upon us to respond, we cannot be limited by past responses, conventional wisdom, conditioned reactions, memory or received teachings. We must engage with what the circumstance demands and with what is required.

When we are mired in expectations, desiring things to be as we like, or fearing that they will be what we dislike, our response becomes rigid. Unable to simply do what the situation demands, we hesitate, frozen, as we attempt to determine how to bend the situation to our will. The self desires predictability, so that we can control the situation towards its desires. It is only when we operate naturally, the self diminished, that we actually act, energy flowing to where it is needed. The less we operate from the self, the more dynamically we respond to conditions with flexibility.

Flexibility can be practiced; we begin by considering myriad views, never limiting ourselves to a single view. If we are used to looking at something from the front, we also then take it in from behind. But go further and consider the sides, the top and the bottom. Perhaps look at it from a distance, up close, or constantly rotating. If we always experience something while seated, stand up. Move closer, stand on a chair, consider it from just outside the room.

We look at our thoughts, feelings, memories, inclinations and instincts in the same fashion. We consider every angle, question everything. We accept that there are endless views, each of which has its own lesson to impart. We do not give in to preferences, to likes and dislikes, to grasping or rejecting.

All views do not have the same utility, but will offer multiple perspectives. It is essential to not fall into the trap that all views are equal. Looking at things from all sides simply gives a more diverse picture with greater nuance. But in the end we need to respond decisively with what the moment requires.

Operating in this way with all things, thoughts, events, and experiences, will cultivate ever greater flexibility.

Immediacy

If we hesitate, we are lost, distancing ourselves from what is really going on. Our default orientation is towards the constructed self—how we are perceived, what is the best answer, what are the key alternatives, and what's our best move. These various ways of gaming out our response to circumstances are all in service to the false notion of a self which we take as separate, isolated and permanent. This "self" is only intent on its own preservation, and on reinforcing this delusion.

When we respond with immediacy, we learn to bypass the filters of the conditioned self. We don't dither, unnecessarily weighing some hypothetically perfect response. If someone falls in front of us, we help them up without consideration of how we may appear, what others may think, and how it will benefit us.

We can practice immediacy in all circumstances, simply by responding without thought of the self. This shouldn't be contrived but a natural act. The self can latch onto this, projecting false spontaneity, making it into an identity. We move counter to this tendency by acknowledging mistakes, and repenting for the transgressions caused by self-oriented behavior.

As we practice this, it becomes increasingly less mediated by the self. It becomes effortless and natural.

A good friend can help us in this endeavor via encounter. We can pose questions to each other that demand an immediate response from original nature, eschewing conceptual and self-oriented gestures. This can be informal, two friends batting questions back and forth, or with more rigor, where we engage in investigation over a period of multiple encounters until our responses arise naturally.

The myriad conditions bring us endless encounters with people, circumstances, and beings that demand a response. As we increasingly sidestep the trap of centering everything toward the self, we respond more and more naturally, with greater and greater immediacy. Over time, self-centered behavior becomes less dominating and we move through circumstances as water flows around rocks, as it cascades downstream.

Uncertainty

Certainty is the death of practice. When we decide that we have come to the bottom of things, that there are no further depths to plumb, that we know how things are, we stop looking. We cease investigating. When we conceptualize our insights into words and language, it never is able to express *what is*. It is always insufficient and even more problematically, it turns those insights into an object that we desperately grasp onto. The self craves security. The fundamental impermanence of things is what leads the self to try to hold onto what it likes, and push away that which it does not. Certainty is always a strategy for the self to hold on, to grasp onto understanding, feeding into our ego as an "awakened" self.

Uncertainty, by contrast, is the nature of things. The nature of reality is impermanence, an infinite network of causes and conditions. When we look ever deeper, beyond the causes and conditions, nothing can be found that is fixed, that is changeless. This emptiness itself is fundamental reality, the essence from which things arise. To see into this is not an experience that we can hold onto and conceptualize with words. Thus not-knowing is what remains. We can embody this understanding as the functioning of original nature. But all the ways that we try to concep-tualize the nature of reality are always insufficient. Thus, the very nature of things is uncertain and the very understandings that the self relies upon are inad-equate. For those who allow original nature to flow freely, who doesn't divide the world into self and oth-er, this not-knowing is not a barrier, but *what is*.

Equanimity

When we do not orient our actions around our-selves, we are functioning from equanimity. The root of all of our delusions is the sense that we are a sepa-rate entity moving through this world. We respond to circumstances by trying to hold onto what we like and push away what we don't like. Grasping after perma-nence, desiring to abide in a place where there is only what we desire, the ever shifting impermanent nature of reality confounds us and brings us nothing but dissatisfaction. When circumstances go our way, we desire for this to continue on, greedily grabbing as much as we can, wishing for ever more. When cir-cumstances turn against us, we react angrily, pushing away what we dislike, desiring nothing more than its immediate cessation. In this way, we are always out of balance, pushed this way and that by circumstances and increasing the overall discontent in the world.

The Dream Mountain Way is one of equanimity, of being immovable by circumstances. We respond to circumstances genuinely, and with humility, but we do not allow them to push us around. We are not ob-structed by circumstances in the world or of our own creation. Feeling things fully, we are not ruled by anger or desire. This is the path of moving through the world without obstruction.

We practice equanimity in all that we do. We acknowledge the core delusion of a false sense of separateness and thus avoid operating in service to that delusion. We are content with all that we have and accept circumstances as they play out. We act, but not from delusion. We acknowledge and learn from our mistakes. When we act, are we trying to hold onto what we regard as positive circumstances? Are we running away, rejecting that which we don't like? We question our preferences, and look for the contradictions. When an activity promotes the self, we reorientate it toward others, or as simply being a part of what is going on. When a strong sense of distaste arises, we question that. What is it that we are recoiling from? We spend time with that which is uncomfortable.

Everything is complete, in and of itself, and trying to shape it to our preferences is the road to suffering. Accepting that things are the way they are and transforming our own views, this is the Dream Mountain Way.

Attentiveness

There is only what our gaze is upon right now, at this moment. When we dwell upon the past or speculate on the future, we lose this immediacy. To directly respond to circumstances without mediation is to live fully engaged. We use our memories and our abilities to speculate as tools when the circumstances require it. But to run our immediate experience though the filters of the past, to game out possibilities, to gnaw on experiences, to endlessly consider alternatives, is to feed the constructed self.

We develop attentiveness by being fully present in our bodies. We are not an operator of this body, a disembodied consciousness steering this flesh bag through the world. We feel our entire body. We are aware of its constituent parts, its feelings and sensations. What is the sensation of movement? How do we feel when sitting? We observe closely the sensations aroused with physical activity. We do this without labeling sensations, parts of the body or actions. We do not engage in commentary on our activity or sensations. We do not discriminate or otherwise distance ourselves from the sensations. We simply act and are aware of the sensations in our bodies.

As we become ever more present, observing the sensations of our body, we embrace attentiveness in all aspects. We monitor our thoughts in the same way. In stillness-sitting, we are always engaging in this practice by noticing when we follow wandering thoughts, when we are disturbed by aroused feelings, and when we are no longer present with the practice we are working with. We notice this. We observe as the thoughts, feelings, and emotions fade away. As our facility with this practice develops, we are able to observe stray thoughts as they arise and fall away. This is attentiveness.

In all our actions that we undertake, we stay present by engaging entirely with the task at hand. We cultivate this ability through single-tasking. When we are eating, we just eat; when we are sitting, we just sit; when we are working, we just work. We eschew mental commentary in these actions, the running narrative that distances us from circumstances. In all activities we are fully engaged in what is really going on, moment by moment.

The practice of gazing in all its myriad forms is to be engaged precisely in this way. What is in front of us right now—when walking, when sitting out of doors, whatever the sensory input may be—we just let it come in, and allow our attention to naturally fall on what is in front of us. If we find our thoughts moving into the past or dwelling on the future, we direct our attention to our abdomen. Stop. Breathe. We open our awareness to our whole body, allowing what is in our field of view to seamlessly shine in. We are fully engaged in where we are right now, with what is really going on.

Connections

Gazing deeply into things, the self recedes. We see through myriad layers. We find a lack of anything fixed, unchanging, or permanent, that exists in and of itself. At the heart of all things, there is no heart. There is only change. Everything is brought into existence instant by instant, due to a direct cause or indirect conditions. Likewise, everything is only a cause for another momentary expression of this flux. Everything is interconnected and dependent upon everything else. Absent these connections, nothing remains, but through these connections, all things arise.

When we sit in the still pool, we can see this generative process in the arising and falling away of thoughts. If we simply let them arise, they persist and fall away, coming from emptiness and returning there. They are not an independent object, existing outside of us. Thought follows thought and outside of these thoughts is only emptiness.

Gazing deeper still, we can see that emptiness and phenomenon are views into *what is*. Seeing into the emptiness of things, that absence of anything essential, is seeing into *reality as is*. Seeing phenomena in that emptiness, likewise, is reality. There is only *reality as is* and nothing can be outside of it. In accordance with that, there is a truth of discrimination into form that is just as valid and, equally, must be embodied. Even accepting change, our limited view is of objects coming into being, persisting for a time and then fading away. But the reality is that there is only change, only the process. It is the process that is real, that is true.

From a deep, embodied understanding of this truth, we can then see deeper into the nature of reality. Change is the essence. All things are expressions of this, and we can see how phenomena are, in essence, all the same. While their manifestation is instant-by-instant transforming, endlessly varied by causes and conditions, their fundamental nature—change—is always the same. Thus in essence, everything is the same.

Likewise, everything can be seen to be dependent on any other thing. There are only temporary expressions of the infinity of infinite connections, but isolating any given expression, we can see how it is the cause of all the other expressions. It is like an infinity of mirrors, all reflecting each other. From any given mirror, we can see all of the other mirrors.

Furthermore, like the images in these mirrors, the images, which in and of themselves are transitory, and dependent on all of the others, we can see how they freely interpenetrate. That is, no image in the mirror obstructs any other. This is a view that we engage in throughout the gazing practices, which in themselves, are insights into this realm of connections.

The essence of it all is that we are able to function without that sense of a separate identity, without forcing discrimination upon things, and without distancing ourselves as self and other. All things are not only dependent upon all other things but interdependent upon them. All things are the same in essence, yet unique expressions of this infinitely complex, shifting web of interconnections. That there are no fixed elements, that things are not permanent and unchanging, means that no condition is permanent. This means that we are able to let go of delusions, to see through the separate self, to not be pushed around by thoughts, feelings and emotions. Change is only possible when things are impermanent.

Experiencing reality in this way, as not separate, but instead, dependent upon all things—seamless with the web of interconnections—we are truly free. We are no longer trapped in views, and limited by a self that we take as permanent and unchanging. We take everything as it is, in essence identical, a constantly shifting flux in the infinity of infinities that is *reality as is*. Then we simply flow through this world.

Empty Awareness

When we are rooted in our direct experience, our internal monologue falls away and we are just operating as awareness. Awareness is the functioning of *reality as is*. This is being in tune with original nature—simply pure awareness expressing itself through our provisional forms, through our bodies. When our sense of identity is rooted in our original nature, this is empty awareness. Normally, our identity is centered in a sense of self, which is an amalgam of memories, feelings, and conditioning. When we are able to see through our conditioning and let go of it, this sense of the separate self is seen as fundamentally empty. Empty awareness is what remains.

As the commentary falls away, there is a sense of an immense silence. There is a great power in stillness and out of it seeps this great silence. Silence is the experience of empty awareness. When we begin to embody this modality, it begins to seem like a roaring silence. All of the practices described herein are devoted to this silence, to pure empty awareness.

There is nothing that abides, unchanging, and independent of original nature. Everything is dependent on everything else. There is a lack of anything permanent, independent, or unchanging. When we are open enough, we can know this intimately. Thoughts rise and fall. The seasons spin through their cycle. Things are born, live and die. When we fully realize this, and embody this, we have begun the process of opening to *what is*.

As we begin to fully embody this flux, this impermanence, we can slip past the bounds of our conditionings—past the constructed self and encounter *reality as is*. This encounter is within the realm of the conditioned, the realm of flux. But it is this unmediated experience of reality that is open awareness. The deeper we engage in the practice of letting go, the less support there is for the constructed self and it is increasingly constrained, and understood as a provisional conglomeration. When the self is no longer able to reconstitute itself, then there is no-self, just empty awareness.

Traces of conditioning still remain; the functioning of reality is not *reality as is*. Deeper practice, and deeper investigation leads to even the letting go of the mind of empty awareness. What remains is *reality as is*.

There are only then expressions of totality, constantly in flux, interconnected and interpenetrating.

Reality As Is

There is only reality, nothing separate from it, no source, no realm above or below, or anything beyond *what is*. It cannot be grasped by the conceptual mind, cannot be adequately described. Any attempt to do so is simply vague allusion, metaphor and hand-waving. But we ourselves are not separate from it and so if we are able to put down the constructs we have formed, that sense of a separate self, then there is, in the immediacy of being, totality.

All true practices and methods are entirely oriented around dropping the barriers that have been erected, and working through the conditioning that is the self, until there is just *what is* and not that sense of self and other. For only then can we really grasp even the pointings and metaphors used to try to give a flavor of reality. This is not an experience. That is simply the past. It is not past, present or future. It is *what is,* inexpressible and beyond any experience. When it is all boiled down, it comes to the fact that we must see it for ourselves.

When we speak of the "nature" of a person, we may use words like curious, energetic, cheerful, melancholy, exuberant etc. These are not things, they are the nature of a thing, the way it expresses itself.

When we speak of original nature or *reality as is*, it is like this: not a thing. All of the things in our experience–form, thoughts, feelings and so on–are all in constant flux. A thought arises, persists for a time and fades away (or spawns another thought). A person is born, lives their life (perhaps spawning another life), and then dies. The seasons begin with burgeoning life in spring, fecundity in summer, aging in autumn and fading away in winter. We see that everything follows this cycle: atoms, molecules, feelings, viruses, insects, animals, cities, machines, planets, stars, and galaxies. But what is it that persists, that isn't subject to this birth and death? Only that fact, that everything is in flux–is dependent on all things, is, in essence, a process. This process is constant, unchanging and fundamentally empty. This process is the nature of all things.

Totality

From another angle, we can observe that everything is dependent on other things. People beget children; a thought begets another thought; a plant comes from a seed, from the sower of the seed, from the soil, from water, and from sunlight. Where do all these things come from? They come from their own web of conditions which, in turn, come from their own web of conditions, repeated ad infinitum. It is not so difficult to see that any given thing arises because of all things. Everything is interconnected. If we could sever all of the connections, what remains? Nothing. Visualize a dense web of threads. Reaching into the center of the web and pull all the strands away to the edges. What remains?

This then, is reality–the permanent, unchanging, all-pervasive nature. But recall what nature is: it is not a thing, it is not a substance, it itself is empty.

But this emptiness is not different from that total interconnectedness. They are, in fact, simply two ways of looking at it. Two sides of the same coin. Because the nature of all things is this emptiness, there isn't any obstruction between things, nor in their essence is there any fundamental difference. Thus, all things interpenetrate. From the point of view of any given thing, there are all things. From the view of all things, any given thing can be isolated.

Openness

The functioning of this totality is openness (or awareness), another word that has little meaning outside of direct knowing. We can attempt to consider this indirectly, to hint at this. When we hear a sound, what is that which hears? When we see something, what sees? When we focus our attention, what is it that we are focusing? There are many methods to investigate this and truly, that is the only way. The moment by moment experiencing of sense data, of thoughts, of feelings—not the things in themselves but the experiencing of them—this is awareness. When there isn't that collection of thoughts, memories, and emotions that we identify with, when we are empty of all identities, then the functioning of reality flows through us. Many people have experienced a limited form of this when so deeply engaged in an activity that their sense of self recedes or even seems to temporarily vanish. Then we are just doing the activity, functioning freely.

When we are engaged in genuine practices, we have periods where we drop all of these identities, encounter reality directly, and we are in the condition of empty awareness. Empty of self, we are purely functioning. Our conditioning—the embedded identities—bring back the self over and over again. And so we keep practicing until this experience becomes embodied. That is, we have fundamentally changed ourselves. This is wisdom, the embodied understanding of *reality as is*. The expression of this wisdom is compassion. When we intimately know the interconnectedness of all things, and when we drop the identities that lead to our alienation, anxiety and distress, we naturally wish for all to be in this freedom and this wish becomes our primary motivation.

Expressions of *what is*

In the realm where most people operate, this wisdom and compassion manifests through our lived experiences, memories and personality. These can all grow and deepen as wisdom and compassion become increasingly embodied, as they make up our individual expression of reality. Thus, in the conditioned realm, this manifests as curiosity, creativity, love and so on. These expressions differ dramatically from the orientation of an individuated self. From the point of view of the self, curiosity is *"I want to know,"* but when expressed from wisdom it is wonder and joy. Likewise, creativity manifests in service to the self: *"See what I've done, how artistic, or clever, I am."* Love, even when genuinely for others, is always rooted in the self wanting itself to be loved. But from wisdom and compassion, creativity is an expression of reality itself. Love is naturally truly selfless. Without grasping onto the recipient, there is true and boundless generosity.

This is how reality manifests itself from the stance of individuation. Reality, as it is, is conditioned; it expresses itself in the myriad things. For the nature of things is dependent on things, just as things are dependent on this nature. We can never work through all of our conditioning, for our conditioning is what we are. This is why these expressions are always individual, why there is no "path," why we are never "done." In our lives, we work through what we can, always digging deeper, becoming more and more true to *reality as is*. The more we drop the artificial barriers, and discard false identities, the more freedom we find. We increasingly move through the world without obstruction.

See it for yourself

None of what is written here should be taken on faith; we must see this for oneself. This is the driver, the motivating force: to encounter *reality as is*. We make various attempts to try to convey some of the flavor, but we struggle to say something beyond what it is not. No words ever truly suffice. We can attempt to describe some of the ways it manifests in the conditioned realm, manifestations that people can see in others. But all of this is to inspire and encourage that dedication to seeing this for ourselves. We use method after method to try to find what works for us. Quickly, this can become form, habits and then ideologies and systems. All of these are things that are not it, that we will then have to let go of.

Ultimately, it comes down to not-knowing. We can never conceptually bring this, "being an expression of fundamental reality," into the limited realm of conditioned thought. But there is a knowing we have when we have embodied this "being an expression of fundamental reality," that is beyond words, that manifests in all our actions, and in our lives. In the end, it is simply the need to experience it directly and a process to help facilitate this. Even that process erects barriers that must be dropped, but the process is necessary for most of us. Everything that arouses and inspires that need to know must be abandoned as soon as possible. The more we can put down now, the less we have to put down later.

Patterning's like this are merely an attempt to encourage us to put it all down and encounter reality directly. For only then are we able to resolve that most essential question, of *what is true?*, and, *how then do we live?*